IT'S WHAT MAKES ME... ME

A RETIRED ATTORNEY'S RELATIONSHIP WITH LIFE AND TIMES

MARK SHAIKEN

Mark Shaiken

Copyright © 2024 by Mark Shaiken

All Rights Reserved

No part of this book may be reproduced, stored in a retrieval system, or transmitted by any means, electronic, mechanical, photocopying, recording, or otherwise, without written permission from the copyright holder other than the inclusion of brief quotations embodied in articles and reviews. *Unless otherwise indicated, all the names, characters, businesses, places, events, and incidents in this book are either the product of the author's imagination or used in a fictitious manner. Unless otherwise indicated, any resemblance to actual persons, living or dead, or actual events is purely coincidental.*

Published by 1609 Press LLC
Denver, Colorado

ISBN (print) 979-8-9908537-0-6
ISBN (ebook) 979-8-9908537-1-3
Library of Congress Control Number: 2024912982

Cover design, interior layout, and proofreading by *Damonza.com*
Copy editing by Debbie Burke, Queen Esther Publishing LLC

First Edition
Printed in the United States of America

It's What Makes Me . . . Me - A Retired Attorney's Relationship with Life and Times

To all my family, friends, colleagues, past, present, and future. You've made me what I am, for better or for worse, and I hope you feel it was mostly for the better. Thanks!

Contents

A Little Context 1
1: Why it is What Makes Me . . . Me? 3

Some Stuff About Me 7
2: I Look Bad in a Hat 9
3: Ramblin' Not Amblin' 12
4: No Rainbows in the Closet—Just the Hammer & the Nail .. 16
5: Color Confusion 24
6: Music & Me (Redux) 28
7: Baseball & Me 31
8: Lefties & Me (aka Basketball & Me) 36
9: Backing into the Hydrant—The Big Lie 40
10: Learning To Trust 46
11: Shake It, Bake It, Anyway You Make It (Nicknames & Me) 49
12: Is There Always Meaning? 54

On Writing 65
13: Why Write Books? 67
14: Just Write 70
15: Paperback Writer 73
16: The Quest for Readers 76
17: You've Published—Congrats!!—Now You're Reading the Reviews. Why? 83
18: Just My Two Cents—Filtered 90
19: The Struggle to Belong—The Ode of an Outsider 93

Ice & Snow 97
  20: The Attempted Assault, Battery & Theft—Much Ado About
      Nuthin' 99
  21: Tobogganing & Long-Term Relationships 105
  22: "Kill Him!!!"—The Case of the New England Whalers Game
      Incident. 109

Pop Culture & Me 113
  23: No Satisfaction & What You Want & Need—My Request to
      Mick and Keith. 115
  24: Lennon & McCartney 120
  25: Vinyl Records Are Back? I'm Sorry. When Did They
      Leave? 123
  26: Guitars & Me 129
  27: Tremé—The City with a Storm in Its Future and a Twinkle
      in Its Eye. 133
  28: Spiderman & Iron Man 137
  29: Bionics—Steve Austin, Jaime Sommers (. . . & Me?). 140
  30: Masters of the Air. 146

Observations, Reflections, & Opinions 151
  31: We Know What You Had for Breakfast 153
  32: Shaking the Ketchup Bottle—Bringing Back the
      Anticipation. 158
  33: I Can't Keep Up 162
  34: Let the Darkness Out. 167
  35: Wins & Losses 169
  36: Lessons from the Northeast 173
  37: Those Low-Down, Nasty, Good-for-Nothing COVID-19
      Blues 176
  38: Laughing Instead of Crying & Other Things My Nanny
      Said. 179
  39: The Empty Stadium. 183
  40: Saving Us from Ourselves—Bomb Drills at Manor Oaks. . 187
  41: The Legend of Honey Haverford 190

Aging–We All Seem to Be Doing It **195**
42: I'm About to Be Old 197
43: When All My Strands Are Gone.................... 203
44: Getting Old—The Golden Years Scam................ 206
45: Doesn't Anyone Want to Be My Doc? 211
46: Using the Calendar to Avoid the "Look" 217
47: My Time 220

Employment & Me................................ **223**
48: The Bagel Bakery (The Case of the Forklift & the Rolling Bagels)................................... 225
49: The Long Drive Contest.......................... 230
50: The Aptitude Test............................... 235
51: Work, Sleep, and Repeat.......................... 238

The *3J Legal Thriller* Series **243**
52: You Go Girl: The Story of 3J and Her Series 245
53: One Foot in Front of the Other—William Pascale....... 249

Poetry & Me..................................... **253**
54: A Little Poetry Context 255
55: Blue Sky Afternoon 256
Don't Ever Change................................. 259
Emily M'Love 261

Some More of the Law & Me....................... **265**
56: Once Upon a Time, I Was an Attorney 267
57: Teaching Law—What Was I Thinking? 271

Wrapping It Up.................................. **277**
58: Tying It All Together 279
59: Ralph Waldo Got It Right (Be Yourself)............... 281

A Little Context

1
Why it is What Makes Me . . . Me?

IN 2020, I wrote and published *And . . . Just Like That—Essays on a Life Before, During, and After the Law.* After publication, I appeared on many podcasts, and hosts interviewed me about my career pivot from my days going to bankruptcy court to writing. Some asked, "How did you go about writing the book?" I answered, "It sort of wrote itself over forty-one years during which I entered the law field, practiced law, and then, eventually, exited."

Do books write themselves? Until the podcasters posed the question, no one had ever asked me that before. Before *AJLT*, I had co-authored two bankruptcy books, so I was damn sure books didn't write themselves. It was a labor of love but lots of work. Work I confirmed I loved.

No, of course, *AJLT* didn't write itself. But I had lived through the experiences, felt the feelings I had felt, had the stories to tell, and all I had to do was organize my thoughts and type. I didn't have to create. I just had to explain everything in an approachable, interesting, sometimes thought-provoking style.

After *AJLT*, I started my 3J Legal Thriller Series. My protagonist is a Black female bankruptcy partner in a large Kansas City law firm. In the series, I had to invent—stories, characters, plot twists, tension, and resolution. A galaxy I created out of whole cloth and imagination. I added a touch of nonfiction history; realistic courtroom scenes, legal process, and dialogue; Kansas City BBQ; and jazz, Kansas City style, all mixed together to form my literary gumbo.

This was a fresh experience for me. Fiction. I had never written fiction. Well, not unless an occasional judge had read something I wrote in a legal memorandum, disagreed with the argument, and deemed it fictional.

Oh, for the good old days.

Now, I'm four books into the 3J series: *Fresh Start*, *Automatic Stay*, *Unfair Discrimination*, and *Cram Down*. As I researched for the fifth—*For Cause*—I realized that before and after *AJLT*, I had written many other essays. Some I've never published, and others I shared only with a small audience. I've now added more essays and organized them in this collection I call *It's What Makes Me . . . Me (IW3M)*.

My essay process is simple: I have things on my mind, I write them down, you read them, and in doing so, I transfer my ideas to your head, and I move on to the next topic. Writing things down gets them out of my brain, hands them off to you, and leaves more space in my head for new stuff. I don't have a monkey brain chattering away at me all the time, but I have lots of notions in there and I share them. Sharing things is my way of trying to figure it all out.

Some information about *IW3M*.

First, if you've read *AJLT*, you'll remember it ends with me riding down my work elevator for the last time, and when I reached the lobby, I was no longer an attorney. It touched briefly on what the post-law life held for me. It didn't discuss in any detail that writing would occupy a good portion of most post-law days. So, for those who wondered what I've been up to since *AJLT*, besides 3J and her little entourage, I offer *IW3M* as my second book of essays.

Second, when I practiced law, clients paid me to tell them what I thought. Old habits die hard, and now that I'm a civilian again, writing is my way of letting people know how I look at things. Maybe in my civilian status, they no longer want to know what I think, but to be fair, I'm not certain they always wanted to hear all my thoughts when I practiced law. And if they did, they weren't always happy that they had asked me for my thoughts after they heard what I had to say.

Third, how I look at things is varied. Sometimes, it's funny. Sometimes, it's not. Sometimes, it's pretty. Sometimes, it's ugly. Sometimes, there's a little more law to write about. Most times, there's not. Sometimes, it's about my life and times. Sometimes, it's not. Sometimes, it's about my relationship with life. Sometimes, not. Sometimes, it's a hard topic, a little rough to take in, but addressed head-on (I know you can take it). Sometimes it's light and airy.

I've organized the essays into the following groups: "Some Stuff About Me." "On Writing." "Ice & Snow." "Pop Culture & Me." "Observations, Reflections & Opinions." "Aging—We All Seem To Be Doing It." "Employment & Me." "The *3J Legal Thriller* Series." "Poetry & Me." "Some More of the Law & Me." And "Wrapping it Up." You can read all or any of the essays in any order you would like, including from start to finish.

Fourth, in *AJLT,* I pointed out that in life, there are head people and heart people. While I always figured I was a heart person, I had been in the law business for four decades and the legal field is the ultimate head game. Perhaps, even as I exited the business of going to court for a living, the head game is still in me, and perhaps the best way to gravitate toward being more of a heart person again is to write it out—my way of working it on out.

Fifth, anyone who's been in the law business for a long time, like me, perhaps, maybe, just possibly, could use some therapy. Consider these compositions my therapy sessions with you. I thank you in advance for the couch and your ear. Send me an invoice and I'll pass it on to Medicare to review and process your payment if approved.

And, last—writing books like *IW3M* helps me find my soul. Just like in *AJLT*, you'll learn a little about what makes me . . . me. Hopefully, you can take it and stand it.

In my new life of not going to court—*My Life 2.0*—I haven't retired. I don't like that word. I've just *re-tired* the treads. In *2.0*, I often consider how I got to where I am and where I'm going. As Amadi Browne, one of the good guys in *Cram Down,* says to his evil brother Jordan, you can't know where you're going unless you know where you've been, a notion Jordan loudly rejects.

The theme of *IW3M* is exactly what Amadi preaches: it's about where I've been, reporting it, honoring it, and, when possible, making peace with it. All of which helps inform me (and now you) more about where I'm going in whatever time I have left in this world.

Here's the thing. I'm not famous. Just an average Joe. But odds are, so are you. Most of us are. We average Joes just live our lives. These essays are about my relationship with my life. Maybe, in some ways, just like your life and your relationship with it.

So read on and see some of what's inside my head, my relationship with life, and what has always made me . . . me.

Some Stuff About Me

2
I Look Bad in a Hat

I don't look great in a hat. But I wish I did. Actually, I look bad in a hat. I wish a hat on my head made me look tough and wise and a member of the pop culture. It doesn't. Why is that? Why do I still use one in some of my author endeavors?

For each book I write, I try to update my biography and my author's picture. The photo ends up on the back cover of the book, my social media platforms, my marketing materials, and my podcast pitches. The life of an indie author: I create and run all of that myself. I enjoy the little business I've created, although it's still true that the difference between an indie author and a pizza is that a pizza feeds a family of four.

My latest Denver photographer is `Jason DeWitt`. I first saw his work at a local art cooperative. Edgy, interesting, storytelling portrait work.

We set up a shoot at his studio and I brought a small ensemble of clothes to rotate through. One was a hat I had picked up somewhere—maybe Walmart around Halloween time. My author hat. The hat I hoped would make me a pop literary icon.

Yeah, right.

I'm not much of a hat aficionado, but I love the way others look in hats. Many of them are my pop heroes. Keith Richards in a porkpie hat; Mick Jagger in a Panama hat; Hank Williams in a cowboy hat; for that matter, any country star in a cowboy hat; Jimi Hendrix in a psychedelic wide-brimmed hat; LL Cool J in a Kangol bucket hat; Dr. John (Mac Rebennack) in a beret; Humphrey Bogart in a Resistol fedora while playing Dashiell Hammett's Sam Spade.

You get the idea. Hats are style. They make the cool look even cooler. They say something about the person. They're the ticket to enter the room where the pop icons all hang out. They add a component to a person's aura.

At least the aura of some people.

P.J. O'Rourke wrote: "A hat should be taken off when you meet a lady and left off for the rest of your life. Nothing looks more stupid than a hat." My modification of P.J.'s observation would be to add that, for many, nothing looks more stupid than a hat. For others, the hat looks great.

I'm one of those many and not one of those others. For me, P.J. got it right. Hats make me look stupid.

Hats are part of pop culture. I guess I'm not. I'm just not Keith, or Mick, or Hank, or Jimi, or LL, or Mac, or Humphrey. I lack the necessary cool whether or not I'm in a hat.

I've always hoped wearing a hat would add an element of grit and mystery to my aura, but neither of those characteristics is the real me. And maybe that's the problem. I want to use the hat as a costume piece under which I hide and not an extension of me through which I shine. I don't want it to define who I am. I want it to mask and then change who I am.

I want the public to wonder, "Who's that dashing young man under that cool hat with his long, curly hair cascading out from under it?" Instead, the public undoubtedly snickers, "Who's that old idiot wearing that ridiculous thing on top of his head and why is he trying to cover his growing bald spot?"

During my years of being an attorney, I wore an attorney's

costume most every day: dark suit, white or blue pressed shirt, and power tie. In court, the costume told everyone I was there for business. But that costume didn't hide who I was; it personified who I was and what I was there to do. It showed respect for the institution, the process, and the judge.

My author hat, however, doesn't personify who I am. It's my attempt to *dream* about who I might be, who I wish I was as I race through my seventh decade on planet Earth.

Don't get me wrong. Dreams are wonderful. So many good things in the world start with a dream. But not all dreams come true, even the good ones. My dream of looking and sounding like Sam Spade hasn't come true. I'm still pursuing my dream of writing as well as Dashiell Hammett. That dream hasn't come true yet, either.

Even when I don a hat, nothing changes.

Oh, you'd like to see for yourself how I look in a hat? It won't be too hard. Surf around social media and I'm sure you'll find that image of me in a hat that's still posted.

Maybe I just haven't found the right hat. Or, maybe I need a hat that I wear above a Jimi Hendrix–style statement: a puffy white blouse shirt, a flowing scarf, bell-bottom jeans, a red paisley velvet jacket, fringes, satin, cool jewelry, and a beat-up Fender Stratocaster hanging from my neck that I might just destroy on stage at the end of a set some night.

Maybe if I wore all those, people would gawk at my hip getup and ignore the hat on the head covering the thinning hair and pulled low over the wrinkling face.

Hope springs eternal, but maybe I just look bad in a hat. Yes. That must be it.

3

Ramblin' Not Amblin'

THE OTHER DAY, I was reflecting on my life. I do that from time to time. I concluded that it's been quite a journey, and I realized that I've rambled, not ambled, through most of it.

Merriam-Webster defines ambling as "an easy gait. A leisurely walk." Hmm. I just don't feel like my life has been a leisurely walk. It's always seemed . . . well, so intense. On the other hand, M-W defines rambling as "proceeding without a . . . direction." Now, that seems more like me.

Amblin'. I just never had it in me. Maybe some lives amount to an easy gait. But not mine. No gaitin'. I blame my lack of gaitin' on several factors. Too much introspection. I'm too much of a loner. I'm too self-conscious. I've come upon too many crossroads presenting too many decisions, and I've spent too much time second- and third-guessing my decisions.

I've lived through too many midlife crises.

Just too many ifs and buts. I envy those who've gone through life truly amblin'. It seems like a good way to go but not my way of doing it, and not the lawyer way to do it.

As I look back, my journey's statistics support that I'm a rambler kind of guy. I've lived in seven states, thirteen cities, and three time zones. I've taken four bar exams, and before I moved on, five states had licensed me to practice law. Ten percent of the states in the Union. I've lived at twenty-one addresses. These are not the statistics of an ambler. These seem like the statistics of someone who is searching for a direction.

The amblers I've met are people always fixin' to do something, but then never doing it and never feeling bad about it either. "Fixin' to do something" was a phrase I learned during our Houston years. Sitting on the front porch on a steamy Saturday afternoon, shootin' the breeze with my neighbor as we both weren't mowing our lawns. We knew the lawns needed to be mowed. We knew we would eventually mow them. But while we sat there not mowing, we were fixin' to mow them. Fixin' was the stage before doing. Fixin' to mow the lawn was as close to amblin' as I've come in life.

The biggest factor in not amblin' was always the lawyer thing (you may remember that I write and talk a lot about being an attorney, now a recovering attorney). I was a business bankruptcy attorney for the better part of four decades.

It's not an easygoing practice area. Lots of stress for clients who can't or won't pay. Lots of problems for loan officers whose management has decided the lender wants its money back immediately. Lots of late-night calls, and in the electronic era, late-night texts. Conveying concern and stress and sometimes a sense of hopelessness.

Many of my clients transferred all that stress and all those problems to me. Attorneys don't have the power of clairsentience. But they're in the business of empathy. Absorbing someone's pain and fear and responding with empathy is hard and can take its toll. Mentally and physically. It's pretty hard to amble along after that kind of transference, especially when it happens at 10 p.m.

Also, to point out the obvious, no clients wanted me to conduct business in a leisurely manner. They didn't want to pay for an easy gait. Who would?

Clients expected and paid for purposeful, serious attorneys.

They wanted all the legal maneuvering to be choreographed. They never wanted their attorneys to amble through a legal matter.

A bankruptcy attorney didn't have to be a pit bull in a suit (although many were, including me sometimes), but clients expected and paid for strategy and implementation and staying one or two steps ahead of the other side. They wanted seriousness, a sense of purpose, promptness, and a style that said, "I have your back. I'll get right on your problem and I'll get it right."

Nothing amblin' about that.

Judges also never seemed to tolerate a great deal of casualness, complacency, and easygoing presentations in court. They doubtless figured an easy gait was a sign of a lack of preparation and respect for the legal institution and the courts.

No attorney would ever stroll to the podium and, in a moment of informality, address the court: "Hey man, how's it going, Your Honor?" It would draw the judge's ire. It would engender snickers from the attorneys waiting for the court to call their case.

Eyebrows would rise.

No. If you're in court, you're expected to stride purposefully to the podium and say, "If it pleases the Court" with respect, dignity, and a sense that what would follow was gravely serious.

But despite all the institutional seriousness built into the legal system, at some point I figured out that, theoretically, an attorney could be precise and serious while still having some semblance of a personal life that might seem easygoing.

An *ambly* personal life, to coin a word.

An easygoing personal life wouldn't necessarily have to interfere with going to court and representing a client admirably.

Two lives. The effective attorney life that was going on at the same time as the private, easygoing life, seeking purpose, meaning, trust, and belonging. The things everyone wants in their personal life as they try to figure it all out.

The attorney could do both. Right?

Well, *theoretically* the attorney could.

But I just never seemed to. I spent my personal lifetime sometimes ramblin' around but never amblin'. Occasionally confused. Sometimes lost. Often not separating the law life from the personal life. No actual plan in my personal life; my personal life was my law life. Not unusual for an attorney.

So no chance for an easy gait for me . . . until I moved on.

Now that I've moved on, I have an easier gait, and I even have a plan. I don't have two lives. I'm still decompressing from the attorney gig so I'm not yet perfect at this leisurely walk thing, which is why I don't quite amble. Maybe someday I'll get there. Someday soon. Just not yet.

Without ramblin' through this analysis too much more and without showing too much leisurely gait in thinking this through, suffice it to say that I'm all about rambling, not ambling, through life because that's what I've always done and what I've always known best.

4

No Rainbows in the Closet— Just the Hammer & the Nail

THE STORY OF the hammer and the nail isn't a new one. It's been around since man invented tools . . . and since we learned to be insensitive.

It's the tool and the fastener. You raise the tool, bring it down hard onto the fastener, driving it into something—often a piece of wood. And then repeat. After several strikes, the body of the fastener disappears into the wood, leaving only the shiny head flush with the wood.

But it's also a life metaphor. Sometimes, we dish out pain to others—the hammer. Sometimes, we absorb the impact—the nail. We're human, so it's nuanced even as the moral is clear enough: sometimes, you dish out the punishment. Sometimes, you take it on the head.

Either way, it's always quite painful to be the nail.

Here are a few hammer and nail stories. You'll get the idea.

What Makes Me . . . Me

I was a senior in high school in 1973, rocketing toward graduation and my ticket out of New Haven, Connecticut. The senior prom committee announced the details of my class's prom. The prom song would be "(Take to the Sky on a) Natural High," a beautiful rhythm and blues number penned by Charles McCormick (Charlie Mack to some) and performed by his group, *Bloodstone*.

I loved the song. It was a great selection. I figured it would make a great slow dance number for any senior prom.

It did. I heard about how great it was later. I didn't go to the prom. Too much of a social event, and I had no girlfriend or date. Guys went to the prom without a date, but that would've been a bridge too far for me.

But the prom I didn't go to has little to do with this story. Remember, this story is about the hammer and the nail.

New Haven was (and is) a pizza mecca. Thin Neapolitan pizzas baked in coal-fired brick ovens built in the 1920s by Italian immigrants who brought the oven design and the art of pizza to New Haven. The capital of the mecca was (and is) Wooster Square.

While my folks loved Wooster Square, the extra mile and a half they'd have to drive to get there and the waiting lines to get into the restaurants led them to find a closer, less crowded pizza joint to frequent. For them, it was Whalley Pizza, a blue-collar gathering place on Whalley Avenue—a northwest to southeast major artery in the city.

Again, this story isn't about the greatness of New Haven pizza or Whalley Avenue. Just the hammer and the nail. Here it comes.

We were at Whalley Pizza one Friday night, waiting for the pizza to arrive at the table. I was quiet. Often, we were a speak-when-spoken-to household. No one was speaking to me.

We sat in a worn, vinyl booth, and I nursed a birch beer—a non-alcoholic, clear-colored, relative to root beer popular in New Haven's pizza joints. A wonderfully sweet soda that went great with pizza. There were three of us gathered around the table that night.

I'm not sure where my brother was off to, but he was lucky he wasn't there.

I was comfortable with the quiet at the table. Dean Martin played in the background—"That's Amore." It was à propos as Dean crooned about a pizza pie and the moon in the sky.

There were maybe twenty tables with families in various stages of ordering, waiting, or eating. It wasn't a big pizza joint, so if anyone spoke loudly, everyone in the place could hear.

"You know. It's okay if you're gay," my mom said with volume so everyone in the restaurant could hear. And they did.

She looked at me as she spoke, so I deduced she wasn't telling my dad it was okay if he was gay. Just me.

"W-what?" I stuttered.

"I just need to know if you're gay," she demanded.

Remember . . . it was 1973. Gay people sadly filled closets everywhere and stayed there with their folded rainbow flags to avoid public disclosure and condemnation. People were uninformed and intolerant. Disclosure during those days was not good for employment, education, and a host of other societal conundrums.

"It's okay if you're gay. I just need to know."

Ahh. There it was. Permission to be gay from my mom. She presumed she had the power, like a Catholic priest, to provide me with absolution. Of course, that would mean it was a sin she was forgiving, and it wasn't and it isn't.

By now, of course, everyone in the restaurant had heard her. Many in the restaurant had turned to get a glimpse of the table where a mom was talking to her gay son. A few snickered and shook their head as they drank their Hull's Beer, the beer that never made New Haven famous.

All I did was blink. No other body parts worked, all frozen in a lockdown. Today, we might call it an operating system crash.

Our pizza arrived at about the same moment as my mom gave me her blessing. The server, who had waited on us before, put the pizza down, made no eye contact, and hustled off. She was pretty.

What Makes Me . . . Me

We had seen each other before. Before that night, maybe she had entertained the idea that someday I'd ask her out on a date. Then she heard the absolution, adjusted her expectations, and left. Maybe she felt sorry for me. Or maybe she felt lucky she avoided interacting with—God forbid—a gay person.

The pizza sat there in the middle of the table.

"Naomi, cut it out," my dad finally said.

"What? I just need to know."

"Why do you need to know?" I asked, surprising both my mom and my dad.

"What?" she asked, surprised I hadn't answered her question. I guess she had suspended the speak-when-spoken-to rule, and now there was a complete ban on speaking, except to answer the question posed either yes or no.

"I'm not gay, but why do you need to know?"

"I'm your mother. I just have to know."

"No, you don't. It's really none of your business."

Luckily, we were in a public place when I pushed back. Lord knows what she would've done if we were home. I spoke loud enough for the other diners to hear. Today, they may've applauded me. Back then, maybe they plotted to beat me up behind the restaurant after dinner.

"Why do you think I'm gay?"

Now she had regained her footing and was in control again. "You don't date. You don't talk to girls on the phone," she said belligerently. She wasn't used to someone challenging her.

There was more discussion. I may've pointed out that public discussion like this didn't make dating easier. I may've said it was hard to have a girl call me at home when Mom would answer, "Shaiken residence. Fuck Hoover. How may I help you?" Kids at school wondered if I lived in some kind of crazy house and didn't want any part of it or me. They had told me that.

But those weren't the reasons I didn't date. I had a very complicated home life and couldn't imagine injecting a girl into the mix. I was just waiting to go away to college. There, I figured I could find a girl to hang out with. That was my plan.

You might say I'm the hero in this story. You might say that because I pushed back, I was the hammer and my mom was the nail that night. But you'd be wrong.

I inflicted no pain. She did. She suffered no damage. I did.

It was a night of public humiliation for me. Remember, again, it was the early '70s. I had no use for public humiliation. No high school kid would. I prayed no one in the restaurant that night went to my high school and could report on Monday that Shaiken was gay.

So that night, I was the nail, and my mom, with no filter whatsoever, was the hammer. It was a role she was quite used to. While she might have said under oath in a court of law that she meant no harm, that night, she took a big swing at the nail's head and connected solidly, bending the head slightly as she drove the nail deep into the wood.

Leaving just the bent head for all to see and chuckle at.

I never returned to Whalley Pizza before graduating from high school. I know I never went there after I graduated. I favored Sally's Pizza in Wooster Square.

Still do.

≈

Saturday, September 20, 1975. I met my soul mate, Loren, in my junior year in college, at a Saturday "mixer" where we danced to very loud music and could barely hear each other. It wasn't "Natural High" playing, but that was more than fine. I had moved on from high school prom issues. I didn't need "Natural High" to bring any of them back.

At the end of the dance, I asked Loren which dorm she lived in and she said Merion Hall. In 1975 at Bryn Mawr College, you had to know the dorm a coed lived in to call them on the phone. There was a central phone system in each dorm. When you called,

What Makes Me ... Me

someone answered the phone. You told them who you wanted to talk to, and they buzzed the student to come to the "Bells" room to take the call.

Sunday, September 21, 1975, 10 a.m. I called Merion and asked the operator to read me the names of the coeds who lived in the dorm. It was so loud at the mixer that I didn't hear Loren's last name. In truth, I wasn't sure I had heard her first name clearly, either.

After a pause, miraculously, the operator read the names alphabetically, and when she got to "Laura B," I said, "That's her. Can you buzz her, please?"

Minutes later: "Hello?"

"Hi, Laura. It's Mark Shaiken."

"Who?"

"We met last night at the mixer and danced."

"I'm afraid I don't know you. I didn't go to the mixer. I was studying in my library carrel last night."

"N-no. We danced together last night."

"Is this a prank? I'm going to go now."

Click.

Ooh. I didn't see that coming.

I called Merion back and asked the operator to continue down the list. When she got to Loren Cody, I said, "Yes. That's her. Can you please buzz her?"

I'm sure the Merion operator was as suspicious as could be, and I'm sure if this had all happened in 2024, I wouldn't have gotten any names of coeds who lived in Merion. We're much more safety- and privacy-conscious today than back then.

"Hello?"

"Did you go to the mixer last night?" I dispensed with introducing myself.

"Who is this?" she countered.

"This is Mark Shaiken. Did you dance with me at the mixer last night?"

"Yes. Hi."

Oh, thank God.

※

A few weeks later, I took Amtrak home to New Haven to discuss the budding girlfriend issue with my mom. A phone call wouldn't do.

I had waited for this moment for a long time. In the living room, I said, "I have a girlfriend."

"Oh, I'm so relieved. Thank God! Alfred, did you hear that?"

"Thank God? What does that mean? Didn't you just say it was okay if I was gay?"

Silence.

"Look, I didn't come home to have another discussion with you about being or not being gay. I'd like to bring Loren home for fall break for you and Dad to meet her."

"*Mazel Tov*. Wonderful."

"Here's the thing. If you dare say anything—anything at all—to her, that would cause her to never talk to me again. Anything! Then you and I are done. Do you get that?"

There would be no hammer and nail between Loren and my mom. We needed to get that resolved. That was the point of my visit.

"What kind of way is that to talk to your mother?"

"It's the only way to talk to you. I need to have your solemn promise on a stack of Bibles that you'll be on more than your best behavior. *Capisce?*"

Capisce (ka-pish) is slang for "do you understand?" It derives from Italian and Latin, but my mom believed it was Yiddish and adopted it. She knew very well what it meant.

"Alfred, do you hear what I'm hearing?"

This was a common tactic my mom used when she wanted to be the hammer. Misdirection. Talking to someone else about me as if I wasn't in the room.

"Don't you talk to me that way, young man."

Discussion over. She didn't answer the question.

Later that night, my dad came to my bedroom and told me he'd handle my mom and I should bring Loren home for the midsemester break.

Handle my mom? Was that even possible? If he had that superpower, why the hell hadn't he used it more often? But I took him at his word. He was my dad.

※

Loren and I went home for break, and my mom was fine. Better than fine. Loren became the daughter my mom never had.

But that's not the point of the story.

The weekend I came home for the discussion, I was the hammer, and my mom was the nail. That relationship rarely happened. She didn't much like it.

But my dad privately enjoyed it. He had been the nail so many times his head was flattening out; he may have taken some pleasure in seeing that weekend play out.

Like I said, in life, the hammer and the nail metaphor is nuanced.

5

Color Confusion

MARC CHAGALL OBSERVED: "If I create from the heart, nearly everything works; if from the head, almost nothing." I'm pretty sure I'm a heart guy.

Nothing represents the heart in all of us more than art. Art expresses emotional content created to evoke an emotional response. My relationship with art is easy to explain. For me, art is photography (see *https://markshaikenphoto.com*). Here's why.

My high school required me to take an art class before junior year. I ignored the rule. You see, I'm colorblind and the prospect that I had to attend a class and create colorful art for others to critique totally freaked me out.

While I've capitulated and use the common word "colorblind" to describe myself, I'm not a fan of it. I'm not at all blind. I can see just fine. A better phrase would be "color confusion" because the true problem is I can't tell the difference between some colors. But, since the world says I'm colorblind, that's the word I'll use here (under protest).

Adults discovered my colorblindness in second grade in New Hyde Park. My classmates and I were supposed to draw our teacher with crayons, and I drew my teacher's dress in blue. Apparently, everyone else saw she was wearing a pink dress. She may've been. I couldn't tell.

My teacher assumed I was being a smart aleck for drawing a blue dress, and she hustled me first to the principal's office for a confab and then to the nurse's office to make sure I had contracted no illness. It was that nurse, and I wish I could remember her name, who took out a colorblindness test, gave it to me, and noted in her journal that I flunked. When you're colorblind, the six to seven million cones in the macula of your eyes don't work properly.

Color blindness tests are ingenious, but for those of us who are colorblind, they're also insidious. The test is a palate of small, colored dots, hundreds of them. Embedded in the maze of dots is *supposedly* a hidden number.

If you have color skills, you can see the number. If you're colorblind, you can't. Just that simple.

I've never seen a single number in the array of dots in my entire life.

I suggest there's a number "supposedly" embedded in the dots because I've considered that maybe there's no number hiding among the dots. Maybe it's just a grand conspiracy perpetrated by billions of earthlings aimed to degrade the approximately 300 million people worldwide who have some colorblindness.

I'm not paranoid; I'm just saying.

Because of this minor affliction, there was no way I'd take a high school art class and subject myself to the usual questions: What color does this look like to you? Answer: What color does it look like to *you*? Question: Can you see that the orange is orange? Answer: I know it's orange, but my orange looks different from yours. Question: Do you see everything in black and white? Answer: Good question, but . . . no.

Remember. It's not, in truth, a blindness. It's color confusion.

This is the best way to explain what I see and what I don't see. My dad purchased his first-ever color television in 1971. A small-screen Panasonic. He told me to tune the color for him manually (no auto-tuning in 1971). The booklet said I should find a football or baseball field, tune to the greens, and once the greens were right, all the other colors would fall in line.

So, I found a Mets baseball game on TV and tuned the Panasonic greens. But I saw little difference between green and orange, and while the greens looked great to me, my dad came in and exclaimed, "The damn thing doesn't work. Everything's orange!" A lesson to the wise: never have your colorblind son tinker with the television color.

So, of course, I declined to take a high school art class. But rules were rules, and the principal said a not-for-profit organization had arranged a trial black and white photography class at my school. He told me the class would fulfill the art requirement and asked, "How about that?"

I said yes; I took the class, fell in love with the art of photography, and the rest is history.

Almost all my photos from the era before digital images were prints and slides. I kept them on the top shelf in the closet in my second-floor bedroom when I went off to college. After I departed for college, somehow the images made their way from my bedroom closet to the basement.

From here, the story gets a little murky and the facts are, to say the least, just a little sketchy—the prints and slides all disappeared. The story my parents told me was that while I was away at college, there was a flood that destroyed everything in the basement, including the pictures.

Wait. Flood? I didn't hear about a flood. Basement? Wait. How did the images get down there? It's a mystery, for sure. But what wasn't a mystery was the loss of thousands of images, negatives, and slides.

I'd like to say that losing my art was so devastating that I went to law school and then tried bankruptcy cases for four decades, but I fear that would be way too simple an explanation.

Since 1977, when I discovered the aftermath of the alleged

flood, I've been on a mission to make all new images, better and better, more and more, and save them on hard drives and clouds in many secret and secure locations. I make images to this day, and it's an integral part of my life. I shoot sports, portraits, landscapes, macros, places, things, music, politicians . . . pretty much anything.

And the colorblindness? The camera and I have a deal. I take care of subjects, composition, and creativity, and the camera takes care of the colors for me. The camera does a much better job with the colors than I can. I confirm this from time to time because I've tinkered in Photoshop to make a blue sky bluer. After adjusting the sky to my liking, my wife looked at the picture and asked: "Did you use some kind of crazy filter on your lens? The sky is purple." Purple and blue, like orange and green, look the same to me.

Oh well. No color editing for me.

Photography was my saving grace during my attorney years. I could turn to my heart and lose myself in photography when I seemed lost in the practice of law, and that helped me find myself, if that makes any sense.

The dual existence of photography and law sometimes confused my partners—an attorney who shot sports or a photographer who tried cases? No matter. I'm grateful I had photography during my law years. Every attorney needs a place to retreat when law and law firm life becomes overwhelming. I have several attorney photographer friends. I believe they'd concur.

And now, I have my writing and photography.

Hard to beat that as long as I don't tinker with the colors.

6
Music & Me (Redux)

I wrote about this topic in AJLT. I decided to revisit it here. Music 2.0. Here is some more on the topic.

As a kid, I played the piano. It was a nonnegotiable requirement imposed by the household powers. I'm sure I'm not the only one in America with this story. Piano was my mom's idea. She was something of a concert pianist and had designs for me to be the same.

Ha!

As a child piano player, I performed at recitals from time to time. My last piano recital was in 1965. I was supposed to play Stephen Foster's "Beautiful Dreamer" at a fundraiser for our New Hyde Park Cub Scout Pack No. 125.

That fundraiser was a combination of comedy and musical performances. The Pack advertised the evening in the *New York Daily News,* which even carried my picture.

That night, someone official announced my name. I strode to the piano in my bow tie and sports coat, bowed, and took my seat on the piano bench. My mom and my piano teacher sat in the front row.

What Makes Me . . . Me

For reasons I still don't fully understand, I played "Beautiful Dreamer" fast—very fast—and instead of a lovely 9/8 piece to be played in *moderato*, I played the entire song in less than fifty seconds, as speedily as my little hands would allow. My 1960s ska version of "Beautiful Dreamer," I suppose.

Just like the pianist in *Reefer Madness*, I played like someone possessed me. And when I finished, I bowed to the audience of a couple of hundred people in the Manor Oaks Elementary auditorium, and you could hear a pin drop for a moment. The moment seemed like an hour.

No one could figure out if I was part of the comedy or the musical portion of the show.

The audience decided I was in the comedy troupe, so they laughed. Then they applauded. Loudly. They loved it, even if it wasn't supposed to be a funny piece.

My mom and my piano teacher glared and then shrunk.

My mom didn't talk to me for a week. It seemed like a month. When she finally did, I announced that my performance of "Beautiful Dreamer" was the last time I would play the piano. Ever. And it was.

You see, I was in the midst of a debate of sorts with my mom and my piano teacher. I wanted to play Beatles songs. What ten-year-old in 1965 didn't?

I told them I wanted to play "I Want to Hold Your Hand." The answer was a hard "no!" In fact, on February 9, 1964, when the Beatles appeared on *The Ed Sullivan Show* and the British invasion officially began, my mom didn't permit me to watch. If memory serves me correctly, we watched a Leonard Bernstein PBS show.

Perhaps my rendition of "Beautiful Dreamer" was my way of saying that when it comes to music, "You're not the boss of me."

Turns out I had much more power in the music negotiations than I ever realized. My first brush with dictating the course of events based on my assessment of leverage. A precursor to life as an attorney? Maybe. Who could imagine Stephen Foster would lead to such negotiation sophistication in a ten-year-old?

A few years later, I found a second-hand guitar, fell in love with it, and have played guitar ever since. I'm pretty sure my mom never wanted to hear me play guitar, except perhaps through the walls.

I'm completely sure she never *asked* to hear me play. She didn't look at the guitar as a musical instrument, opting to view it simply as not a piano; to her, it was a long-necked piece of wood with only twenty-two frets and six metal strings kept in the bedroom that anyone could tune instead of a piece of beautiful, high-gloss furniture with eighty-eight keys and two-hundred-thirty strings kept in the living room that only a professional could tune.

Another moment among many where we would have to agree to disagree.

The point is this: music has always been important to me. For that, I have my mom to thank, despite the disputes. So, thanks, Mom.

Music is also very personal to me. I write music but I don't perform. I guess I'm not willing to risk another "Beautiful Dreamer" incident. Indeed, I rarely play with or for others. At least not yet. It's mine and mine alone.

And my voice is an acquired taste, although, of late, I'm working on that with a singing coach.

During my law life, music was another one of those places to go to escape. Every attorney needs a solid, reliable, and accessible place to go to escape. So again, thanks, Mom.

Maybe someday, I'll show up on a corner at Denver's Sixteenth Street Mall with my guitar. Or maybe someday, I'll show up at an open mic night at the Last Chance Bar and Grill in Denver's South Broadway district. I doubt it, but who knows? Hope springs eternal.

7
Baseball & Me

My heritage, as my parents and grandparents explained it to me: my parents were first-generation Americans, both born to Russian Jews who fled the homeland when the Cossacks *asked* them to leave one night, much like the storyline of *Fiddler on the Roof*. Granting the Cossacks' request, my four great-grandparents left the homeland one night in horse-drawn wooden carts, made their way to a port, and sailed to the New World.

My mom's family ended up in the Bronx and my dad's family ended up in Brooklyn and Montreal. There was little information about either family while in Russia. Because of this, I can't say my Russian ancestors were baseball fans. For that matter, I don't know if anyone in Russia is a baseball fan.

But my family, once they arrived in the New World, were huge fans.

My mom and her Bronx family were vocal Willie Mays/New York Giants fans and Yankee haters, and my dad and his Brooklyn family were avid Jackie Robinson/Brooklyn Dodgers fans and Yankee haters. When they married, there was only one way to address the obvious Giants/Dodgers conflict. They took their vows in Manhattan and moved to Queens—designated by the proper authorities of both families as acceptable, neutral baseball territory.

The only baseball fact the families could agree upon was their hatred of the New York Yankees.

Thus, baseball was in our DNA and properly governed many life decisions. I was born in Queens in 1955, just a month after the Brooklyn Dodgers beat the New York Yankees in the seventh game of the World Series to win their first and only championship while the team was based in Brooklyn. A favorite story my parents told me was that while they listened to the World Series on the living room radio, my mom, then eight months pregnant with me, moved an ashtray and Duke Snider promptly struck out. My dad blamed my mom for the Snider whiff and didn't talk to her for days.

Seemed like a perfectly irrational reaction to a completely rational situation. The Duke striking out? Never. It must've been the lucky ashtray. Who would move an ashtray at such a critical moment?

I wonder if I heard that argument while I was in the womb.

The Dodgers and the Giants left for California at the end of the 1957 season, the Dodgers to Los Angeles when New York refused to build them a new stadium, and the Giants to San Francisco in the hopes that the move could revitalize a ball club that was having trouble drawing fans to their Bronx stadium.

On the last day of the 1957 season, Giants fans stormed the field and the team's public relations officer lamented, "If all the people who will claim in the future that they were here today had actually turned out, we wouldn't have to be moving in the first place."

That was it for a National League baseball team in New York and only the hated Yankees remained. Until 1962 and the New York Mets.

The Mets were perfect for our family. They would ultimately play in Queens, not Brooklyn or the Bronx, solving my family's baseball territory dispute once and for all.

For the Mets' first two seasons, they played in the Bronx at the

Polo Grounds where the Giants had played, awaiting the completion of Shea Stadium in Queens.

I went to the Polo Grounds in 1963 with my New York Giants grandpa and saw Jimmy Piersall play center field for the Mets. My Brooklyn dad didn't go with us. It was a simple decision for him. It was that Bronx thing.

Piersall ran around center field erratically and led the Mets in a loss to Jim Bunning and the Phillies. Fans later learned that Piersall suffered from mental illness, and he wrote, "Probably the best thing that happened to me was going nuts . . . It brought people out to the ballpark to get a look at me."

The Amazin' Mets, circa 1963. I liked Piersall and wasn't aware of his mental illness.

The Mets moved to Queens and Shea Stadium in 1964. With the territory issues resolved for good, my dad took me there several times.

I remember one game we saw Sandy Koufax of the Los Angeles Dodgers give up only a few hits. We sat in the upper deck, pretty far away from the field and the action. But it was still exciting to be there.

The Mets were terrible. They lost one hundred twenty games in their maiden season, 1962. A record that still stands. Records are meant to be broken, but maybe not that one.

Other than the few outings to Shea, I got most of my baseball fix around the neighborhood, playing stickball in the street, collecting baseball cards, and watching the Mets on WOR Channel 9 television. Sponsored by Rheingold Beer. "My beer is Rheingold, the dry beer. Look for Rheingold wherever you buy beer." The broadcasting crew of Lindsay Nelson, Bob Murphy, and Ralph Kiner brought the games to me and figured out a way to talk their way through epic losses night after night.

I watched the Los Angeles Dodgers play the Minnesota Twins in the 1965 World Series in Brooklyn with my dad and my Brooklyn Dodgers grandpa on his black and white Motorola television. My mom didn't come. Remember, in our family, Brooklyn was not neutral territory.

I had Tony Oliva's baseball card and concluded I should root for the Twins. When I cheered for Harmon Killebrew, the Twins' first baseman, my grandpa said to my dad: "Alfred, take him [me] outside on the stoop and talk to him."

The talk was simple: no one roots against the Dodgers in Grandpa's house. Even after they abandoned Brooklyn for California. Lesson learned.

The Mets finally achieved respectability and then greatness when they beat the Baltimore Orioles in the 1969 World Series. Their reliever, Tug McGraw, coined the motto "Ya gotta believe." It was a good time to be a baseball fan.

I married in 1978, and we moved to Topeka, Kansas. We quickly became Kansas City Royals fans and made the hour-long trek from Topeka to Kansas City to watch the Royals play.

This was the first time I had rooted for an American League team. Continuing my family's tradition of sitting in the upper deck, my wife and I would drive like the wind on Friday night after school and work to get to the ballpark, order a few hot dogs, and take our position closer to the clouds than the field.

By the time we signed on as fans, the Royals were excellent. It was the era of George Brett and a cast of other greats. They challenged the Yankees' dominance, and I loved it. In 1980, Geroge Brett flirted with batting .400 and the Royals finally beat the Yankees in the American League Championship Series after three straight losses, only to lose to the Philadelphia Phillies in the World Series. They broke through to beat the St. Louis Cardinals and won the World Series in 1985. We had just moved to Houston but cheered on the Royals from afar.

We remained Royals fans through their World Series victory in 2016 and then moved our allegiance to the Colorado Rockies and back to the National League.

And that's where we are today. Here in Denver. Rockies fans.

What Makes Me ... Me

Hoping the Rockies will realize that every team I've rooted for in my life has won at least one World Series. But I'm worried. The Rockies may be the only team around that could vie to tie or beat the Mets' record of one hundred twenty losses in a season.

I like to believe it's not the "X's" and "O's" but the Jimmies and the Joes that matter in baseball (and life). But to compete (and make it in life), you've got to have the right Jimmies and Joes and good management. Right now, the Rockies don't. All they have is a great stadium with an amazing sunset over the mountains and the only place where, during the seventh inning stretch, the singer sings "For purple mountains' majesty. . ." while the fans cheer.

I love to watch them, but sadly, they may challenge my lifelong love of the game.

8

Lefties & Me (aka Basketball & Me)

THE LEFTIES CLUB is small. *Psychology Today* says it's between 9.3% and 18.1% of the world population and settles in at a likely 10.6%. That means in 2020, there were 827 million lefties in the world. Seems like a lot, but in a world of over eight billion people, it's not.

What am I? A little of both. I mostly reach for things with my left hand. I shoot baskets lefty. I kick lefty. I can bat either way (not well from either side). I bowl lefty. I can eat with either hand but favor my right. I shave righty. I brush my teeth with either hand. My left eye is dominant. When I played golf, I was a righty, but considered switching to lefty. Couldn't hurt. The left side couldn't have been any worse than what the right side gave me on the course.

I write righty but because my handwriting is so poor, I've entertained the notion that there was an edict in first grade that I had to write righty. I drive with either hand, but often, it's the left one. Not sure I'd trust the right one to handle the Tesla sometimes. I play guitar righty, but when you play right-handed, the left hand does all the fretboard work.

What Makes Me . . . Me

As you can see, I'm not a pure lefty. So what is "a little of both" person? "Ambidextrous" is the ability to use both hands with equal facility. Under that definition, I'm not a true ambi. I can't do everything with either hand. Therefore, I've coined a phrase for what I am: a "hybrid ambi." Some things with one hand. Some with the other. As far as I can tell, no one seems to know what percent of the population is a true ambi, let alone a hybrid ambi.

What a *shemozzle*. Shouldn't I be entitled to know how small my club is?

W. C. Fields observed, "If the left half of the brain controls the right half of the body then only left-handed people are in the right mind." I'm not sure I'm in my right mind and maybe even less and less as I grow old, but I appreciate the sentiment.

My major intersection with the art of being left-handed has been basketball, my favorite sport to play and watch.

I had some basketball heroes. Two righties—Walt Frazier (Southern Illinois University; Knicks) and Cazzie Russell (University of Michigan; Knicks). The rest of my heroes were lefties: Dick Barnett (Tennessee A&I College; Syracuse Nationals; Cleveland Pipers; Lakers; Knicks), Willis Reed (Grambling State University; Knicks), and Gail Goodrich (UCLA, Lakers; Sun; Jazz).

And then there was the most famous and prolific basketball lefty of all time: Bill Russell (San Francisco University; Celtics). I respected him on and off the court. He was an amazing man. I wished I could have loved him as a ballplayer. But I couldn't. He wore the Celtics' green.

Other lefties I loved to watch—because they were lefties: Phil Jackson (nicknamed Action Jackson with the Knicks), Nate Archibald, Isiah Thomas, Lenny Wilkins, Jalen Rose, David Robinson, Bob Lanier, Toni Kukoc, DeAndre Jordan (now with the Denver Nuggets), Manu Ginobili, Artis Gilmore, Billy Cunningham (Seventy-Sixers; he was pretty close to being a hero for me), and Dave Cowans (another Celtic).

Barack Obama is a lefty and loves to play basketball. Add him to my list, please.

I actively played basketball from my pre-teens through my mid-fifties. I was a point guard. I wasn't great. What I lacked in skill, I made up in world-class dreams about being great. Nothing better than going to bed with a transistor radio hidden beneath my pillow so I could listen to Marv Albert call a Knicks game: "Reed to Frazier to Barnett—SWISH!!"

Lefties are interesting basketball players. They tend to like to drive to the hoop from one side of the court—the left side. At times, it seems like lefties have no use for the right side of the court at all.

Someone once said, "When nothing goes right…go left." That was me. When I played, I saw two sides to the court. Left and further left. I mean, I could go right and dribble with my right hand and do a right-handed layup. But I always struggled with the philosophical question: "Why go right with all that real estate on the left side of the court?"

I last played basketball when I was fifty-six years old. That was after a six-year hiatus from the game. Six years before, I had cataracts and wore bifocals. I'm here to tell you that basketball at any level is not a game to be played with progressive bifocals. Then I had cataract surgery, reclaimed my vision, and returned to the court to shoot around. That was it. No jumping. No running. No teammates. No games. Just shooting with friends as old as me.

Even just shooting around, the game had slowed considerably for me. But that's okay. Old-age basketball mirrors old age. Things slow down.

In my thirties, my goal was to play at least once in each of my decades. I'm sixty-eight right now and will be sixty-nine later in 2024. I've gotten a partial knee replacement. When that heals up, I'll buy a ball (red, white, and blue to honor the old ABA), find an outdoor court in Denver (one that no one else frequents), and shoot around. No videos. No selfies. Just the ball, the hoop, and me. Mission complete.

When I find that court and shoot around to give meaning to my playing days, I'm sure I'll go left and further left. I'm too old to learn any new tricks. That's what going right for a lefty always seemed to be: a trick. A ruse. An unnecessary distraction. If asked, I'm confident Dick Barnett and Gail Goodrich would agree. I'm sure Willis Reed would have agreed before he passed away.

When it's my time to pass on, I'd like my headstone to read: "Left and further left." Any casual visitors to the headstone who don't know me will conclude it refers to my politics. Anyone coming to visit the headstone who knew me well will know it was the motto of a left-handed point guard.

9

Backing into the Hydrant—The Big Lie

CONNECTICUT ISSUED ME my first driver's license in late 1971. I had just turned sixteen. The new household rule was I could drive my mom's Pinto to high school once or twice a week.

The first time I drove the Pinto to school was also the first and last time I told my dad a significant lie. When I told it, it was almost the end of my teenage experience.

The driveway setup was this: my mom parked her Pinto in the driveway, and right behind it, my dad parked his Ford sedan each night when he got home from work. So my task in my first taste of traveling freedom was simple: back the Ford out of the driveway and park it at the curb so I could drive the Pinto.

7:15 a.m. Here's what I did.

I loaded my books into the Pinto and dropped my basketball in the trunk because, after school, my friends and I planned to play pickup basketball at a court near school. We were having a New England warm spell even as winter set in, and we planned on taking advantage of it before Mother Nature shut down outdoor basketball for the season.

What Makes Me ... Me

I borrowed my dad's keys, got in the Ford, turned the key in the ignition, and the car roared to life. *So far, so good,* I thought.

Leading up to my driver's test, I had practiced about everything a baby driver could work on. Everything except backing my dad's car out of the driveway and parking it in front of the house.

The Ford sedan was a much bigger car than the Pinto, and the trunk was huge. But I was confident. No problem.

I put the Ford in reverse and slowly backed it out into the street. "Careful" was my middle name. Then, I cut the wheel hard to line the car up and performed a parallel park in front of the house. My driver instructor told me I was good at parallel parking. The only problem was there was a yellow fire hydrant in front of our house. That and the huge Ford trunk.

The hydrant wasn't new. It had always been there. I had practiced parking the Pinto in front of our house during driving school, but the Pinto, the car I practiced driving with, had virtually no trunk, so I could parallel park in front without coming near the hydrant.

Not true for the Ford. As I remember the events, the trunk wasn't just huge. It was enormous. I should have considered the size of the Ford's trunk that morning, but I didn't. Planning is always a good idea, but it didn't cross my mind. I was just a sixteen-year-old and, like most teens, specialized in living in the moment.

I plowed the back of the Ford into the hydrant. The sound of the hydrant and the trunk meeting was sickening. Metal on metal. As the Ford docked with the hydrant, I slammed on the brakes and sat there while I tried to figure out what to do. *Could my dad see what happened?* I worried. *Probably not,* I concluded. The kitchen was at the back of the house and that's where he was drinking his coffee. I glanced at the front of the house anyway, just to confirm he hadn't been watching me out of the front windows.

I decided all I could do was to gingerly pull forward, undock the car from the hydrant, finish parking, and bring the keys in. The sound as the rear of the call pulled free of the hydrant was loud and nauseating. I pressed forward and parked. There was nothing else I could do.

"Some days you're the fire hydrant, and some days you're the dog," Peter Conrad quipped. I felt like the hydrant looking at all the dogs in the neighborhood as they approached me right then.

I turned off the car, got out, and didn't look at the rear of the car or the hydrant. I brought the keys in. My dad and I said nothing. He was a quiet person before leaving for work. Just him and his coffee. Maybe pondering his upcoming day and how much he hated going to work. It was always a good idea to let him drink his coffee in silence, but this time, perhaps, was the moment I should've broken the silence and come clean. I didn't. If I had, I was sure that would mean he'd revoke my permission to drive the Pinto to school. I had waited years for this day and just had to drive to school.

I drove in silence, more carefully than usual, with the Ford weighing on my mind. First, I picked up my friend Bruce before heading to Jimmy's house, and then on to school. Bruce got in, rolled down his window, lit a cigarette, and turned on a local A.M. radio station.

"Hey, how's it going?"

"I just backed my father's car into the fuckin' fire hydrant, man. I am screwed."

"Jesus. What did he say?"

"Nothing. He didn't see it, and I didn't tell him."

"You put a big dent in the back of his car and left? And you don't believe he'll notice it? That's your plan?"

I said nothing.

"Man, you are totally fucked."

We got to Jimmy's house, and he hopped in the back. He too lit up a cigarette. Luckily, my mom smoked like a chimney and the car already smelled like stale smoke, so she would never know my friends smoked in the car.

Bruce turned to face Jimmy. "Shakes backed his father's car into a fire hydrant and didn't tell him."

Jimmy's eyes widened, and he gave me three deep belly laughs as he said, "Oh man." He stopped, smiled, and finished, "Are you ever screwed!"

"Yeah, I get it."

"What's the plan?" Bruce asked.

"I have no plan."

"How could you? You're just fucked on the trunk thing. I meant the plan for after school."

I exhaled slowly. "I've got a ball in the trunk, and we can head over to the court and play some hoops. Meet up at the car at 2:45."

"Sounds good," Bruce said.

"And what about the car and the hydrant?" Jimmy asked.

"No idea. I'm totally screwed."

I got home that night just as the sun set. We'd stayed extra long at the basketball court. It was my idea to extend the games. I don't know what I was thinking. Unless I planned never to go home again, I figured I'd have to face the music or worse. I resigned myself that I might as well get *it* over with. Whatever "it" would be.

After dropping Bruce and Jimmy off, I drove home. The Ford was still parked at the curb. Right by the hydrant where I had undocked and abandoned it that morning. *Did Dad call in sick and stay home?* I wondered.

I pulled the Pinto into the driveway. I entered the house through the kitchen door. My dad was sitting at the kitchen table in his coat and tie just as I had left him that morning. As if he had never left. As if he waited for me there all day. He looked at me.

"How'd the day go?"

"Okay. School was school."

"Yeah? Anything else?"

I shook my head and headed out of the kitchen.

"Wait up there a minute," he said.

I waited.

"Anything about the Ford you want to tell me?"

Want??? No, I didn't *want* to tell him anything. "No."

"It has a big dent in the rear. Your doing?"

"Dent? Not me."

He frowned, and it turned into a smile. "Yeah, it is. The dent has yellow on it, and the hydrant is missing some yellow."

Oh no. He had gotten all Sam Spade on me and connected the dots.

I dropped my shoulders, looked down, and said a quick, silent prayer. "It's me. I backed it into the hydrant this morning."

"Yeah . . . of course you did." He said a lot of "yeahs" when he was mad. It was his substitute for "fuck" sometimes. Sometimes it was hard to tell whether "yeah" was "*yeah*" or an F-bomb.

"I'm sorry."

"For backing it in or lying?"

"Well . . . both, of course."

"Yeah." That "yeah" may've been just an acknowledgment. Context was always so important.

"You'll have to pay for it to get fixed."

"I don't have much money."

"Yeah. I know." Another acknowledgment? Probably. He knew the state of my financial affairs.

"What should I do?"

"I got some weekend jobs for you. You'll work it off."

"For how long?"

He nodded. "Yeah. For as long as I say." This one may've been an F-bomb.

"Does that mean I can't drive to school anymore?"

"You mean the Pinto?"

"Right." I would never say "yeah" to him, considering what it might mean.

"Did you crash the Pinto?"

"No."

"The Pinto's your mom's car. That's between you and her."

"Does she know about the Ford?"
"Did you tell her when you weren't telling me?"
"No. I didn't tell her."
"Yeah. . . . Like I said, that's between you and her." Possibly another exclamatory F-bomb.

Wait. He hadn't told her? It was a miracle. I was in the clear. I still had my newfound travel freedom.

I turned to leave.

"Hold up."

Uh oh. Here it comes, I worried. The dad giveth, and the dad taketh away.

"A little advice."

I raised my eyebrows, awaiting what could only be bad news.

"Don't lie to me again and we'll all be fine with this new driving thing."

I nodded.

"I'll back the Ford out for a while."

"K."

A death row governor's reprieve. I never liked the "yeah" discussions with my dad. That's why I didn't lie to him again.

⁂

Later in life, after my dad had died, our son turned sixteen and got the right to drive our Honda Civic. Another compact car with a small hatch. I'm not sure what he was thinking, or if he was, but he drove it off-road and bent an axle. He tried to lie about what happened. My wife was furious. Maybe she had never lied to her parents. I was more measured.

Yeah . . . Some teenage moments stay with you.

10
Learning To Trust

MANY YEARS AGO, I listened to a speech by James Kane, an expert on human connections, during which he spoke about the components of the human condition: a sense of purpose, belonging, and trust, the "Big Three." He gave the speech at one of my law firm's annual retreats and geared it toward institutional inclusivity.

Kane is a leading expert on this topic, and I encourage you to read some of his work. I'm not an expert, and I'm not going to be able to provide you with a detailed analysis of society's problems in breaking through barriers to find lasting inclusivity.

When Kane speaks, he's motivating, and his speech got me thinking about my experience with the Big Three.

As a practicing attorney, a sense of purpose was always the easy one. You have clients. They have problems. You try to help find solutions. The job fills the bill of purpose. Even outside the job, I've always had a sense of purpose, whether it's been writing, playing music, or serving on not-for-profit boards.

But the other two—trust and belonging—aren't so easy. At least not for me.

I've written about being an outsider and not belonging. Now it's

What Makes Me . . . Me

time to address the third component of Kane's speech—trust—the hardest for me.

I remember a particular moment in my law firm life when I was terribly unfair to one of my law partners. He had come into my office to explain a decision the firm had made that would impact me, in my view, adversely. He thought not so adversely. I was upset, and I selfishly focused on the impact on me and not the greater good of the firm. He said the impact of the firm's new policy would not hurt me, and he would make sure it didn't.

Then he said it: he said I should trust him. Without even pausing, I replied, "Trust isn't the first word that crosses my mind when I think of you right now."

Harsh.

I regret ever having made it so personal. I hope he and I are friends today, and if we are, it's completely a testament to his willingness to forgive the unforgivable.

Painful as it is for me to recollect that moment, it's an excellent illustration of how a life of distrust impacts day-to-day life. It's taken a long time, but I've learned that distrust adversely affects others. My distrust hurts people around me.

And it's not all that good for my health either.

But why am I like this? Why do I distrust? That's easy. I was taught to distrust. I was brought up to trust no one.

Is failure to trust baked into my DNA? I've concluded it's not. Distrust is something I can—maybe, perhaps, possibly—unlearn. And, if I can't completely unlearn it, when it bubbles near the surface, maybe I can control it. Maybe I don't have to share my distrust each time with the rest of the world.

I've lived a good long time, so I've had a good long time to figure this out. I've come to these conclusions slowly, but I am glad I have (finally).

I've now identified that which has escaped my grasp for so long: distrust is fundamentally bad.

Yet one of my heroes, Benjamin Franklin, opined, "Distrust and caution are the parents of security." I've come back to this quote over the years and longed to talk to old Ben about it. If he was still around to field questions and have a dialogue, this is how I imagine that discussion would go.

"*Ben, if I trust no one, are you saying I'll feel more secure?*"

"*Correct.*"

"*Are you saying a life of distrust has made me feel secure?*"

"*Correct.*"

"*Hmm. That may not be a healthy way of going through the day, Ben. In fact, if the only way to feel secure is to distrust others, what a sad state of affairs we find ourselves in.*"

"*Indeed.*"

It's difficult to talk with a dead guy, even one who's larger-than-life like Ben Franklin. But when I can, even in death, he can be a conversation starter and a thought-provoker.

One of my other heroes is Ernest Hemingway. He had a very different outlook on trust: "The best way to find out if you can trust somebody is to trust them." Hemingway's premise was much more straightforward: make the leap. Show some faith in your fellow humans. Trust them.

Ernest was wise.

Of course, I don't know if he developed his notion of trust before or after a morning of drinking rum with the boys in a Havana bar, but history suggests he may have also done some of his better philosophizing at the bar as he barked, "Another drink, barkeep."

So, to all the people I've distrusted in my life, whether for good reason or for no reason, I offer a very late, past due, generic, but genuine apology. It's so inadequate at this point, but it's all I can do. And to my hero Ben, I respond, "To distrust without good reason is not a good prescription for security. It's an antisocial act. Rather than provide security, it ensures isolation."

Who would ever want to hang around with someone who distrusts you and who readily tells you so?

Barkeep, another glass of rum, please.

11

Shake It, Bake It, Anyway You Make It (Nicknames & Me)

My last name is Shaiken. I've been called Sh-eye-ken. Shanken. Shaiker. When people mispronounce it or get it totally wrong, I correct them by telling them it's simple: it rhymes with bacon.

The story I'd always heard at family gatherings was that when my great-grandfather got off the boat and eventually made his way to the front of the Ellis Island line, an official didn't understand the Russian last name my great-grandfather uttered. So, on the immigration papers, the guard filled in "Shaiken."

My first name is Mark. It doesn't rhyme with anything useful to a writer, but it's an easy enough name to read and pronounce. Other than deriving from Mark the Evangelist and invoking the controversy of whether Mark wrote the Gospel of Mark or whether someone else wrote it anonymously, it's not a terribly interesting first name.

I've had a good number of nicknames in my life. Most of them I like. I'll answer to any of them. Many came from my childhood friend Brian, who seemed to be on a mission to find the perfect nickname for me. During hot summer days after playing stickball in the street, we'd sit under an oak tree and he'd conjure up possibilities. It was fun to listen to him conjure. He was good at it. He liked to link possible nicknames to something he had seen or learned.

I wasn't as good as he was at the conjuring game. So he was just "Bri" (rhymes with eye) to me.

Here are the main nicknames he came up with and some others associated with me.

Maples: Maypo was a maple-flavored instant oatmeal cereal that came out in the 1950s. It was the brainchild of someone at the Maltex Company of Burlington, Vermont. The animated television commercials introduced us to Uncle Ralph and a young kid, Marky, who, after tasting Maypo, whined to his Uncle Ralph, "I want my Maypo." Too cute.

Brian wasn't a big Maypo fan. But, there was a logic to the nickname he worked on. Marky. Mark. You can see the free association. But "Marky Maypo" was four syllables. Brian was a marketing genius and knew four syllables were two too many. So, he shortened it to "Maples," his combination of Maypo and maple, and it stuck.

I was Maples in stickball. I was Maples in Little League. I was Maples under the oak tree. I was Maples, and I liked the name. Just fresh enough that kids who didn't know me needed an explanation, and Brian was happy to accommodate. Just unique enough that no one else in town answered to it. It was mine. Just me.

Maples stuck until we moved to New Haven. No one in New Haven ever called me Maples, and I was fine with that. Brian designed it for stickball games in the streets of New Hyde Park. It served no purpose in dodging traffic and people with bad intent on the streets of New Haven.

Even though Maples stuck, Brian was always on a quest for new, better, more innovative nicknames.

Shake 'n Bake: This was a seasoned breadcrumb coating that General Foods introduced in 1965. I was nine going on ten when it first landed on the grocery store shelves.

It was a bag-based coating. You put the protein in the bag along with the mix, shook it, and baked. I remember it as salty, but it cut down on the time our moms had to spend in the kitchen, so it was 1960s-style progress.

Before we left for New Haven, Brian, always on the lookout for a new nickname, tried to adopt this one for me, but it was a mouthful. You could just yell out "Mark" or "Maples" and I'd instantly answer. Or you could yell out, "Hey, Shake 'n Bake" and I'd answer, but it was three times as many syllables as "Mark." It was a playful way to get my attention but not a sound marketing idea, so it wasn't a keeper.

Shake 'n Bake stuck to food but not to me as a nickname. That didn't deter Brian.

Shaken Not Stirred: This was a line from the James Bond movie series. Brian's parents would take us to the drive-in movie theaters dressed in our pajamas to watch current movies.

Not too many drive-in movies these days. So, for those not in the know, it worked like this: the adult would pay the car admission, we'd pull into a large lot and park in a spot next to a pole on which sat a wired speaker. The adult would hang the speaker from a car door window rolled halfway down, and, like 1960s magic, we had sound. We watched the movie from the back seat, looking through the front windshield to a gigantic movie screen in front of the lot.

Most nine-year-olds didn't have a great idea of what was going on in the Bond movies. But Bond was cool, the special effects were cool, any drive-in was cool, the British accents were cool, and Bond always won and that was cool. It was great to be with a friend on such an early version of a road trip.

Bond loved (and loves) martinis, and he's famous for ordering them "shaken, not stirred." When Brian heard that, he floated the Bond line as a new nickname. I liked the idea of having a spy-related nickname, but four syllables were still a problem for those in the promotion business. Technically, it was another food nickname, although I'm sure people would debate in which food group a dry martini with a green olive served to a British super-spy would fall. But it was food, nonetheless, so Brian's food streak continued.

Shake-A Pudd'n: Shake-A Pudd'n was a dessert item from Royal Pudding whose commercial hit the airwaves in 1966. The commercial had a Beach Boys or Jan and Dean impersonator band singing: "Here's a new kind of pudding you can make. It's called Shake-A Pudd'n, and all you do is shake it." The "it" seemed out of place to me and ruined the rhyme with "make," but I guess someone in the Royal Pudding marketing department was uncomfortable if the ad failed to explain *what* the consumer should shake. So, shaking "it" made the final cut.

I didn't know too many kids in New Haven after we moved there, but like in New Hyde Park, the few I did know wanted me to have a nickname they selected, so they tried to adopt this one as mine with the same problem as Shake 'N Bake. The syllable count.

The New Haven crowd wasn't as marketing savvy as Brian and spent too much time trying to make it stick. It didn't, and I was without a New Haven nickname until high school basketball time.

Lefty: There was one kid on my high school basketball team in New Haven who called me Lefty and still does. A point guard. Ricky. Red hair. Great playmaker.

He was a year older than me. Technically, I played on his team, not the other way around. I liked that nickname a great deal and readily answered to it, although, for whatever reason, it never stuck. Its principal purpose was to break the food streak, for which I was grateful. Food-based nicknames were great before my teens, but a simple "Lefty" to take my place among left-handed athletes of the past was much more appropriate for a teen.

Interestingly, few famous left-handed athletes had the nickname "Lefty." Phil Mickelson, the PGA golfing legend, does. Lefty Gomez, a famous baseball pitcher, did.

But others didn't. Randy Johnson, Hall of Fame pitcher, isn't called Lefty. He's the Big Unit. Babe Ruth was the Bambino. Wayne Gretzky was the Great One. Ted Williams was the Splendid Splinter.

What Makes Me . . . Me

Lou Gehrig was the Iron Horse. Stan Musial was Stan the Man. George Brett was just . . . George Brett. And so on.

I genuinely liked Lefty. Thanks, Ricky. I wish it had caught on.

Shakes: This was my college nickname. Streamlined to follow Brian's two-or-fewer syllables marketing strategy, and it stuck.

I have no idea who came up with this one. It doesn't refer to any food or left-handed predispositions, and it's still my nickname today. I answer to it promptly. No one at my law firm ever called me Shakes. In fact, no one I met after college called me Shakes. But my college buddies still do, and maybe as I get older and more forgetful, that's how I'll be able to remember them: if they call me Shakes, I'll know I went to college with them. Then all I'll have to do is try to remember their name.

Shakey: My wife, Loren, invented this one after we first met in college during my junior year. It's a derivative of Shakes, and as far as I can tell, she's the only one who calls me Shakey.

It's familiar, and it's hers alone. As it should be. It's nice to have one nickname she invented and she alone uses.

At some point, she got creative and called me Shakey Bake. Luckily, she abandoned that name after a short while. She may have gotten feedback from Brian. I don't know.

But as I get older and more forgetful, I'll be able to remember that if a woman calls me Shakey, the odds are pretty high that she's my wife.

Then, all I'd have to do is remember her name . . . . And mine. I should be able to tell my name isn't really Shakey, but will I remember that it's Mark Shaiken (rhymes with bacon?)

Hopefully, it'll all fall into place and won't be too confusing. But do ya see, Brian? Don't you see? What did you start under that oak tree?

12

Is There Always Meaning?

This piece was hard for me to share. I'm comfortable sharing most everything that happened in my life, but until now, I haven't shared what I call "handsy" moments in my upbringing—those times my parents disciplined, or more accurately, took out their frustrations on me. Times were different back then. Many parents disciplined their kids by spanking or worse. My parents went beyond discipline at times as they struggled with their own problems. Hands didn't teach lessons. They were just the means to vent frustration. It's taken me a long time to realize my folks weren't bad people. But my reaction to the "handsy" moments lingers. It's time I feel okay to share this. It's as "About Me" as it comes. Some pieces take time to write and then rewrite. This one didn't. Once I started, it just flowed out.

~

I look back to the different phases of my life and try to find some meaning to make sense of the things that led me to where I am today—which is mostly a good place.

But I've learned that sometimes, it's not possible to find meaning and make sense. Sometimes, there's no real meaning, even as the fallout from the events remains baked into what makes me . . . me.

When there was no meaning and no sense to be made, it just was what it was.

❧

I was a kid in Queens, 1955-60. I was too young to be anything other than a tiny, very young kid living at 40-60 Elbertson Street. There was an alleyway between our building and the next. One day, I wandered away from my mom into the alleyway and got pushed and punched by some older kids. My dad bought me boxing gloves and tried to teach me how to defend myself. I learned some of it, but I hated it.

A month after the alleyway incident, I went to P.S. 89 for kindergarten and at the end of the school year, my folks said my teacher criticized me on a report card because I played with dolls under a table during playtime.

My folks attributed meaning to the boxing and the report card. I don't. No real meaning. It just was what it was.

❧

I was a kid in New Hyde Park, 1960-65 until we moved. I played pickup baseball and football, went to Manor Oaks Elementary School, practiced hiding under my desk during bombing raid drills, joined Cub Scout Pack 125, played little league, secretly listened to the Beatles, hated classical music, didn't want to play piano, had lots of friends, seemed to be well-liked, and I had a black Schwinn that I parked in our rickety garage at the back of our property at 1214 Terrace Boulevard.

I rode that bike to school and used it to race around the neighborhood with friends. Terrace Boulevard to Dallas Avenue to Leonard Boulevard to Evergreen Avenue and home. I ran in to grab

Yoo-Hoos for my friends and me, and then we repeated the circuit. Every night after dinner, when the weather was nice.

No Manor Oaks report cards flagged that I played with dolls alone under a table. I was no longer a loner. I was a part of a community. My friends.

Then we left.

My folks attributed no meaning to the move. I do. I was in the early stages of becoming a social bee. It was a great feeling. Friends and a social life make you happy. I lost most of that and still struggle today to recover it.

∽

We moved on December 10, 1965, and our address changed to 1565 The Boulevard, New Haven, Connecticut. We rented the first floor of a three-story Victorian-style home; we called it the flat. I never met the landlady who lived upstairs, and I only knew her kids by their first names.

In New Haven, the pace of growing up sped up and my status as a kid seemed to melt away into whatever comes next when you grow up too fast.

The household became a source of high volume, high tension, and frequent arguments among the adults. The parental units poorly handled the interstate move they had instigated. As they devolved into unhappiness, they became more handsy with me. I had no friends, and the kids I met at Beecher Street Elementary School, my new school, were a tough crew.

As part of some kind of initiation club, the I Club, they pushed me to the ground and beat me up. I remembered a little of the fighting back lessons from Queens, and I learned the art of tripping your aggressor. Most importantly, I learned I was faster than most of the I Club members. Despite prior formal and in-the-moment training, I wasn't much of a fighter, and when I didn't outrun them, the kids in the I Club, girls and boys, collaborated and beat me up on my walks home pretty regularly.

The kids in the Queens alley had introduced me to this same social issue, so it didn't come as a total shock. I figured some kids are just prone to getting beat up. Ironically, on some days, I ran from an I Club beating to a "handsy" parent at home. Not much of an improvement, but there were no real options for a ten-year-old.

I went from being an "A" student at Manor Oaks to getting straight "Ds" and "Fs" at Beecher Street. No time or interest for studies when you're running from a beating. Interestingly, no one seemed to care about the grades. The parental units had their own issues, and the school seemed to be one of those punch-in-and-punch-out-the-time-clock places for kids. As long as I wasn't truant, no one seemed to care.

The living accommodations in the flat left something to be desired. Someone broke into it several times. Often, the invader took nothing. The evidence pointed to someone unknown who had rooted through drawers and moved stuff around. Sometimes, however, personal property went missing, so I came to hide my toys before leaving for school in the morning. The break-ins always seemed like an inside job by someone with the keys to the flat.

Then the announcement came. We would move again.

My poor fight record wasn't why we moved because I didn't share with my parents what was happening. The move probably had something to do with the break-ins.

It was 1966. I was back to being a loner and now running for my life from time to time, trying to fend off the occasional assault from within the home and without.

My folks decided the meaning was they could end the break-ins—and they did.

But I see a different meaning: I learned that being alert and fast have their advantages.

☙

Our next place of residence was a six-story apartment building at 226 Fountain Street, across from the Sheridan Middle School in the Westville neighborhood of New Haven. I transferred to Davis Street Elementary School for sixth grade and the 1966-67 school year. This was my fourth elementary school. Davis Street was a safe, well-run public school, and I enjoyed my time there. No initiation club. A baseball field and basketball courts for the kids to use over lunch hour. My classmates were welcoming.

But I was only there for one school year. By that time, I was wary of making friends because the lessons I had learned so far had taught me that they would either fall out of my life quickly or turn on me and beat me up. Home life got better, but it wasn't just the "handsy" moments that could change a kid. Turns out that the knowledge of "handsy" moments in the past and the threat of "handsy" moments in the future are just as impactful as the moment of contact in the present.

I played baseball in the Andy Papero Little League and enjoyed that immensely but made no friends on the team. I practiced with them, ran the bases, took my swings, learned the game, and went home. My folks also joined the Jewish Community Center, and I started playing in a basketball league there. I knew little about basketball, but it captured my fancy and still does today.

By then, I had given up piano playing and had just begun to play guitar—a Harmony brand.

I wasn't at Davis Street long enough for my folks to find meaning. But I do. We humans are resilient, and given the chance and a little luck, good things can sometimes happen.

~

We stayed at 226 Fountain Street, and I started middle school in 1967 at Sheridan. It was a tough inner-city school, busing kids in from all over the city. Most of the kids I had met at Davis Street went to middle school somewhere else, so I knew almost no one when the new school year began. The years 1967-68 saw intense Vietnam War protests and riots in the streets and in the schools. It was a time when a young male adult could get a draft deferment

What Makes Me . . . Me

by teaching. So, there were a good number of young adult males teaching at Sheridan who had little teaching experience.

There was also a good number of riots in the school hallways, mirroring what was happening on the streets across America. Riots in school hallways were nothing less than mass chaos as kids ran through the hallways punching, pushing, yelling, chanting, and intimidating—teachers, administrators, and other kids. Lots of hiding in classrooms until the rioters passed further down the hallway. A complete rejection of John Locke's Social Contract and a return to his State of Nature.

Terrifying in many ways, but it didn't differ from the national tension that had boiled over, and luckily, some rioters recognized me and sometimes passed me over, maybe akin to the angel of death in Exodus passing over the Jewish households.

Then Sheridan closed for a period as the National Guard occupied the schoolyard and prepared to put down the New Haven riots and, if need be, the rioters. Men with automatic military weapons lived in green camouflage tents across the street from our apartment and occasionally patrolled Fountain Street.

Around that time, a car bomb went off in the apartment parking lot. The rumor was that the mob commissioned a hit on someone in our building who hadn't paid back his loan. All the windows in our apartment blew out. There was glass everywhere, and it was embedded in the furniture. We all needed new beds. I was outside, down the block at the time. Luckily, none of my family was home.

Mob message sent and received. Bombmaker never identified. Memorable times.

By then, I had some repeating constants in my life: basketball, guitar, the Jewish Community Center. Slowly, I made some friends. Nothing like the community in New Hyde Park, but little by little, the me inside peeked out again, looked around to see if things were safer, and surfaced.

I also had baseball and, suddenly, religion. In my baseball life, I made the Little League all-star team playing first base and got to play under the lights in front of a decent-sized crowd. I tried not to let it show, but the *New Haven Register* ran a small article in which my name, along with the other all-stars, appeared, and I was so excited. My dad even came to watch the all-star game, the only one of my New Haven baseball games I remember him seeing.

Religion seemed to come and go, and as a result, we hadn't had a religious life to this point. We weren't a family of temple-goers or religious practitioners, but we joined a temple so I could study for my Bar Mitzvah. I had to learn enough Hebrew in a year to lead the congregation in a Saturday service.

I always assumed the religious in and out and back and forth was a monetary thing, but it was hard to know and it was hard to have much faith when there was so little faith practiced at home.

My mom got depressed (or perhaps more depressed), and with that, home life devolved. I became more familiar with the wooden square heel on one of her shoes, an upgrade to the customary "handsy" discipline. The heel made it easier for her to dole out punishment. She had no filters by then, so she told me regularly I embarrassed her because I was so quiet and withdrawn. Maybe it made her feel good. Maybe it made her feel in control. Maybe she was right. Who knows?

I stayed away from home during the day as much as I could, arriving back at dinnertime when the arguing began. While the parents attended to their own issues, they weren't "handsy," just later, when they had finished arguing without a clear winner.

By the end of the school year in 1968, I was an almost-teenager playing as much guitar and basketball as I could, wearing well-worn, white, low-top Converse sneakers everywhere, practicing for my Bar Mitzvah, hanging with a small group of friends—Black and White—and, as much as possible, staying out of harm's way in and out of the home.

My folks found this era of social upheaval meaningful, but I was too young to. So, for me, no meaning. It was what it was. Just lots of it.

What Makes Me ... Me

⌘

Two years of Sheridan and then high school. First up, Hillhouse High School in one of New Haven's 'hoods near the 1565 The Boulevard flat. Hillhouse was where Artie Shaw, the famous jazz and big band clarinetist, went. Artie, the musician, had a reputation for being difficult, even nasty. I've heard him say he had a terrible home life. But it wouldn't surprise me if Hillhouse added to the nastiness even though when he went there, it was known as Academic High School.

It certainly had lost that name and reputation by the time I arrived.

Most of the people I knew at Sheridan went to high school at Hillhouse's crosstown rival, Richard C. Lee High School. We lived a block from the dividing line of kids who went to one school or the other. So, off I went to Hillhouse while my friends from Sheridan went to Lee. Perhaps it was the proximity to Beecher, but the school beatings and threats of beatings returned. One time, I had a quarter in my pocket for bus money to get home after school. I never made it to the bus. A group of kids dragged me under a staircase, dropped me to the floor, and kicked me until I gave up the quarter. I ended up in the Yale-New Haven Hospital emergency room and stayed out of school for a week.

Twenty-five cents for a less than five-minute thumping. I wonder if the thumpers divided the quarter among themselves or if the primary thumper kept it all.

I announced I was dropping out of high school and never returning to Hillhouse.

My folks announced we would move to the Lee High School district and I would stay in school.

On this one, my folks and I both found meaning, just different kinds. My meaning was simple: I was tired of getting beat up. I went to school, and it happened. I came home and if I didn't get hit, it felt like I was going to. My folks found meaning in making me stay in school. It was a good thing they did, but it isn't the lesson I take home from this period.

At some later point, as I neared seventeen years old, I told them about my meaning. I'm not sure they got it. They didn't promise to stop hitting me. To them, my meaning was probably just a random view of a kid who had played with dolls in kindergarten.

※

After the announcement, we moved, this time to 59 Alston Avenue, and I started at Lee.

It was a significant improvement. Still a tough, inner-city school in a tough neighborhood, but no beatings, and a growing group of good friends, some of whom I reunited with from the Davis Street and Sheridan days. I still had basketball and guitar. I also had two new loves—writing and photography, spurred on by my English teacher, Rhoda Spears, and my photography teacher, Frank Martin.

It was 1970-73, so there was still the war and civil unrest. Lee was right beyond downtown, and each day, my friends and I walked by the New Haven Greens to get to the bus to take us home. The Greens were home to Yale protests against the war, often led by Yale's own Reverend William Sloane Coffin, a famous peace activist. Lots of draft cards burned, holding hands, and singing "Down By the Riverside (Study War No More)." Lots of arrests.

Very impactful for a young, emerging adult to observe.

By this time, my parents had become so self-absorbed with their own issues that they attributed no meaning to the Lee era. They kept me in school. That was their job. Perhaps that was their meaning.

But for me, Lee had meaning. At Lee, I had friends. I learned to rely on myself for whatever it was I wanted or needed. I became self-sufficient. It wasn't an *it-is-what-it-is* time. It wasn't a meaningless period: I learned I could excel even as I could start to protect myself from whatever was around the corner.

※

Those are some highlights and, where applicable, some of the meanings I attribute to them. Growing up with "handsy" parents, I learned that sometimes they were trying to teach me something in their own way. But sometimes, they were just trying to hurt me, and sometimes they did.

How do I find meaning? I don't. Not always. There isn't always meaning. It just happens. How do I move on and survive? I just do. I've survived, and things have a way of working out for the best. They mostly did for me.

I remember all this for two reasons: first, I have no choice. No kid does. Second, I remember it, so I also remember to hug our kid.

On Writing

13

Why Write Books?

LIFE HAS BEEN a journey of dreaming about writing and putting it off. It was a dream to chase. Sometimes, when you chase dreams, you also get chased by them. During my law career, I had precious little time for either. But I made time along the journey to consider the question, "Why write books?" It took me four decades to come up with some answers, which follow.

Number 1. Writing is better than talking with someone. When you write, you say everything on your mind. No interruptions. No arguments. No debates. No one talking back to you. If you think it, write it. If you feel it, write it. If you believe it, write it. Let the world read it and if they agree with it, bravo. If they don't, either listen and learn or ignore. Either way, keep writing.

Number 2. When you write and put your work out there for all to read, you put yourself out there as well. For us wallflowers, it's the best way to get off the wall. Not without consequences, of course. Some will like what you wrote. Some will not. Those who like it may compliment you. A five-star affirmation and license to continue writing. Some who didn't like your work will review it and explain their negative reaction.

Some of the criticism can help you grow as a writer and a person. Listen to them. They are the path to future affirmation. Some of the criticism will be downright mean. A function of the modern social media era, perhaps. But, it's frankly a little like baseball. If the best hitters in the game are only successful at the plate thirty percent of the time, why do they risk the pain of making an out seventy percent of the time? The hit is worth the quest. As well, the compliment is worth the quest, and the risk of harsher criticism is just part of the game.

Number 3. When you write, looking off into the distance is not a sign of an ill-formed, life-altering pipe dream. No. When you write, gazing and dreaming and drifting are all working. It's part of the process and if it means you're dreaming or even formulating an unachievable pipe dream, it's all good because dreaming, and even pipe-dreaming are part of the writing process. If you are a gaze-off-into-the-distance type, then write.

Number 4. Do you write for fame and fortune? The New York Times bestsellers list? A top ten new release on Amazon? Oprah's recommended reading? An interview with Gayle King on CBS Mornings? A selection by Amazon's Sarah Gelman? Movie rights? Sadly, not at all likely, so no, that's not why you write. Usually, there's no fame and glory. With that in mind, if you still want to write, then you do it.

Number 5. Writing keeps me regular. It's the same as going to work, but it's not a job. It's a pleasure.

Number 6. I have a tendency to get inside my head a bit. Too much analysis going on in there. My law partners noticed it over the years. I blame the practice of law for that. Indeed, no one wants to hire an

What Makes Me . . . Me

attorney who underthinks. Right? I find writing a wonderful way to get outside of my head, and in doing so, share with everyone some of what's in there. I find the share to be strangely soothing.

Number 7. Most of us have opinions. For many people, we have conversations and we say things. All kinds of things. But when we speak, is anyone definitely listening? Are we the tree in the forest that falls, begging the question that if no one's there to hear it, does it make a sound? We make sounds, and we want people to hear our sounds. For those of us who write, we do so to be read, and when we're read, we're heard. We hope that if a reader buys our book and reads our words, they've decided to spend the time to hear us. Not necessarily agree with us. But hear us, nonetheless. Maybe they'll find what we wrote thought-provoking. Maybe they'll come away with a new perspective. Maybe they'll use what you wrote and what they heard from you to make the world a better place in some small way.

Number 8. There are voices in my head. Maybe there are voices in every writer's head. One indie author, M.K. Stabley, recently said that she writes to keep the voices in her head at bay. I don't want to keep the voices in my head at bay. I'm not sure that would work out well for me. They're in there, and the best way to deal with them is to let the voices in my head come out. Make them face the world. Make them take accountability. If I keep them in there at bay, I sense an overcrowding crisis on the horizon. If I let them out, then there's more room up there for thinking.
  I write to free up space to think.

Number 9. So, why write? Simple. Why not? It's a good thing, and we all need more good things in our lives.

14

Just Write

I'm reminded of two quotes when people ask me about my writing habits. "Get it down. Take chances. It may be bad, but it's the only way you can do anything really good." – *William Faulkner.*

"You may not write well every day, but you can always edit a bad page. You can't edit a blank page." – *Jodi Picoult.*

Both are the writer's version of something Wayne Gretzky once said: "You miss 100% of the shots you don't take." Words of wisdom. He is, after all, "The Great One."

Just Write. It's just that simple sometimes. Above all else, get it down on paper. Don't worry about writer's block. You'll have it and it will pass. Don't worry that the words have to be Pulitzer Prize material. They don't. Don't worry that today you weren't profound or prolific. You need not be. Not every day. Maybe never.

How did I come to this motto—*Just Write?* Here's some of the analysis that led to *Just Write.*

When I first sat down to write fiction, my first impression was, "Write some books. Fiction. No big deal." Then I quickly realized, "Wait. Big Deal. VERY BIG DEAL!" Because what did I know about fiction? Nothing.

What Makes Me . . . Me

Then I thought, "K.I.S." Keep it simple. Stop all this endless mulling, weighing, anxiety, and hand-wringing and just start writing. But instead, I needed more analysis. The former attorney thing at work. Analyze. Analyze. Analyze. So then I asked myself, "Why write?" And I realized it was the job description, of course. I told myself, "Writing is dreaming, and gazing, and imagining."

And then I wondered, "But why fiction?" Jeff Daniels answered that for me when he said to someone: "Everything's a story, kid. Stories are what help us make sense of the world."

I would tell stories to help me make sense of the world I live in. And with that, I had done more than enough lawyer-like overanalyzing and I was ready to write.

But I needed a methodology. A routine.

I have some writer friends who wait for their inspiration and then sit down and write. If it means getting up at 3 a.m. to fire up the coffeepot and sitting down at the computer, then that's what they do. Binge writers, I suppose. I'm happy it works for them. Even envious. But that's not me. I'm afraid if I took that approach, I wouldn't binge. I'd write nothing and cringe at my ineptitude. And for me, 3 a.m. is not a time for creativity and clarity.

So I book appointments with myself in two-hour increments. Writing sessions go on my calendar like an appointment because that's how I view them. Appointments with me. My little contract with myself in which I've agreed that I'll sit down at the computer and stay there for no fewer than two hours. If, during those two hours, I write ten words, then so be it. More often than not, however, I key in over ten words. If I'm on a roll, I'll stay over two hours, but no matter what, I'm there for the minimum two-hour session.

I needed this structure and still do.

And dialogue? Another area in which I had no experience when I practiced law. Attorneys talk a lot and write a lot, but they never write dialogue.

Because I didn't know how to write dialogue, I decided to get into character—out loud—and listen to the characters talk to each other. If I just imagine it silently, it doesn't seem to work for me. So, if you happened to wander over by my computer when I'm writing a conversation between characters, you would hear the characters talking to each other.

It helps me keep the conversations authentic. And, anyway, there's some of me in every character. Even the bad guys. So it's good to hear what I sound like when I talk to my alter ego.

Pierce Brosnan once said: "I always see myself as a character actor, but Remington Steele was me. I gave up on trying to be any character. I just put myself as me in this world of Remington Steele and the grand pretender." When I write dialogue, I'm me, the grand pretender, talking to myself and then answering. I even argue with myself.

I write legal and financial thrillers. I want my courtroom scenes to sound the way the courtroom sounded when I practiced law. I want my deposition scenes to sound the way the deposition questions, answers, and objections sounded when I took or defended a deposition. And I want my attorneys and bankers to sound like attorneys and bankers sounded when I interacted with them in my practice.

I want to hear how it sounds to make sure it's real and that I'm not geeking out too much on law and finance.

All of that happens more easily for me if I can hear it playing out audibly.

That's right. I'm the weirdo at the computer who's talking to himself out loud, booking appointments with himself, performing under that contract with himself, and "putting pen to paper," or at least the modern technological version of ink and paper.

So far, it seems to work well for me and keeps me just writing.

15

Paperback Writer

DEPENDING ON YOUR age and musical tastes, you may remember the 1966 Beatles song, "Paperback Writer," penned by Paul McCartney. It can be a slippery slope to try to explain the origins of an idea for a Beatles song. I've heard three explanations for writing a rock 'n' roll song about a writer dreaming of being a dime-store novelist.

In the first, Beatles lore reports that McCartney's Auntie Lil challenged him about writing only love songs. She asked him why he didn't write songs about more important things, suggesting a song about a horse, or a summit, or something else interesting. Later, when McCartney saw Ringo Starr reading a book backstage, "Paperback Writer" came to be, and the rest is history—except for the usual controversies about which Beatle played which parts of the song and whether John Lennon contributed any of the lyrics.

In the second explanation, McCartney reported that as a youngster, he entertained thoughts of being a writer.

In the third explanation, McCartney abandoned the Auntie Lil and career dream stories and instead credited marijuana for opening his mind to the possibility of writing songs about something other than teenage love.

The song presents a writer who sends a letter to an anonymous publisher, hoping to convince the publisher simply to read the book. I presume it's not the writer's first letter to a publisher. The book took years to write; the writer was desperate to find someone to publish the book; the book is roughly a thousand pages; the writer intends to write more pages shortly; the writer can change the story around; the publisher can have the rights; the writer hopes it would make the publisher wealthy overnight; and, sadly, the writer informs the publisher how to return the book if it rejects the submission, even as the writer says over and over that all he or she wants is to write paperback books.

And there you have it. Whether a drug-induced story or one resulting from an Auntie Lil shaming, in his own way, in the mid-1960s, Paul McCartney created a nameless character who captured some of the angst of a modern-day indie author. Turns out when McCartney imagined the longing of a 1960s writer, it wasn't all that different from the dreams of a twenty-first-century indie author.

Don't all of us who write and self-publish just want to be that paperback writer? I do. Don't we just want people to read our books? Check. And if they do, to leave a brief review? Check. We may not say it, but don't we dream every once in a while that a traditional publishing house will latch onto something we write? Check. Don't we long for thousands—no—tens of thousands of readers and reviews? Check. Aren't we willing to change our works around if that's what it takes to fulfill our dreams? Check.

As McCartney's fictional author implored the publisher, I sensed the desperation and related to the ask the writer made of the anonymous publisher: please, please, please just read the book.

How could Paul McCartney have known how an unpublished, or in the modern era, an underread, published indie author might feel?

The answer I came up with is this: he already knew. John and Paul met in the 1950s, started writing original songs together in John's aunt's house, and performed for whoever would listen. They went to Hamburg, hoping to find an audience and hone their skills. They looked for an agent who then looked for a record company. For years and years, no one important would listen to their works, but through it all, the duo kept writing and honing and dreaming. They never gave up the dream. They had resolve. And then, one day, George Martin and Parlophone Records listened.

When I talk with other indie authors, I often hear that resolve as well: keep writing. Never give up. Maybe we self-published writers aren't that different from Lennon and McCartney. Now, to be sure, Lennon and McCartney's teenage dreams came true and then some. They had boundless talent. Few writers I know have quite that kind of talent.

But the lesson is clear to me: never lose faith. Write because that's the calling. Put words down on paper because that's what we're driven to do. And slowly but surely, more people will read those words; maybe not throngs of people, at least not yet. Maybe the throngs will find the next book. Or the next.

After all, all we need is a break . . . because we are indie paperback writers.

16

The Quest for Readers

EARLY IN MY postlaw, new-book-writing career, I foolishly assumed writing books would be the hardest thing I would do. I was so wrong.

Getting people to read the books is way, way harder. The indie author's quest for readers often feels much like Man of LaMancha's "The Impossible Dream."

In the 1990s, I coauthored two bankruptcy law books published by traditional publishing companies—John Wiley & Sons and Aspen Publishing—specializing in publishing trade books.

I never realized how good I had it. All the coauthors had to do was research the law, write the chapters, and deliver them to the publishers. The publishers did all the editing, formatting, and the cover and interior design. And they marketed the books, finding readers to buy and read them. The publishers delivered royalty checks to us that were more substantial than I expected, so I deduced that they were doing a fine job of finding readers.

Back then, there were lots of publishers out there.

Fast forward to today. Before *IW3M*, I wrote and self-published five books (one memoir of a not famous lawyer and four legal and financial thrillers). *IW3M* is my sixth.

What Makes Me . . . Me

Have I eschewed publishers? Not at all. I'd love for Penguin Books or Random House to publish them, just like Wiley and Aspen in the olden days. But consolidation, mergers, and other business pressures have left us with many fewer traditional publishing houses today than in the 1990s, and with the advent of self-publishing, we have many more authors and books.

The law of supply and demand has now infiltrated the world of writing, and the odds of a publisher selecting my books to publish out of the thousands of daily new book offerings is slimmer than quite slim.

Submission of manuscripts is time-consuming and an author like me will surely wait long periods of time for a publisher's decision. Maybe years. I'm now sixty-eight-years-old. I worry if I submit a manuscript to a traditional publisher, I won't get a decision during my remaining lifetime, even if I live to be eighty-five.

And it's so easy to self-publish. Long ago, Amazon perfected the method for any author to publish a book and sell it online. Now, authors can either do it themselves or hire an editor, a cover and interior formatter and designer, and then upload it to Amazon.

I use third parties to edit, format, and design. My little publishing enterprise. Then I upload it myself. Amazon charges nothing to publish the book.

All that writing, editing, formatting, and uploading was the hard part, right? Wrong.

Once I publish the book, I'm on my own to market it and find readers.

There are many outfits who, for a fee, say they'll market your self-published book. The fees vary wildly from hundreds of dollars to thousands and more.

The services don't always make sense. For example, if you sell your paperback book on Amazon for $14.99, the author receives a percentage of the net revenue from Amazon after the deduction of printing and shipping costs. If that royalty for each paperback amounts to around $4 to $5 per book, the author would have to sell two hundred books to break even on a marketer who would charge one thousand dollars to market the book. The math gets incrementally more stark when the marketer charges thousands.

The grim reality is that spending more doesn't equate to selling more.

I have to confess to trying some expensive marketing ideas that were a complete flop. In my heart of hearts, I figured the idea would flop, but I looked at it as a one-time learning experience. Using a marketing service has usually been a losing proposition for me, so I've rejected spending lots of money to hire third parties to market my books. Rather, I've gone my own way.

But I ask myself, "What do I know about attracting readers and selling books?"

I know keenly that the answer to the question is "Not nearly enough."

Through trial and error, I've tried to develop and grow a comfort zone of what I can do without embarrassing myself. Here's what I've settled on (so far) in my quest to find readers.

Speaking: I'll talk to almost any group about my work and my life. I'm always trying to find groups looking for speakers—a speaker series, a local book club, a bar association, a university club, a law firm, etc. I don't expect to be paid to speak. All I need is an audience to listen.

Social Media: I have an active social media presence—for me, *Facebook*, *LinkedIn*, and *Medium*; I have many "friends" on *Facebook*, "connections" on *LinkedIn*, and "followers" on *Medium*. I'm an introvert and a member of the generation that grew up with no social media, but I've learned to be "out there" on social media and I'm a little shameless in serial postings about my books.

For Facebook and LinkedIn, if a book wins an award, I post. I post sample dialogue. I post about characters, including my Emily the Dog character. I post snippets of reviews. I post images of people reading my book. One of the repeating characters, William Pascale, plays guitar and writes songs, ones that I've already written and recorded. So I post my mp3 of the song and tell my social media audience it's what Pascale would sound like if he performed it.

On Medium.com, I write essays, usually one thousand words or fewer, and hope they're interesting enough that readers will enjoy them. If a reader posts a comment about an essay, I always try to respond.

I'm not a regular on Twitter/X. I'm unconvinced that regulars there read books, and if they do, I'm not convinced they buy them. I know other authors find marketing luck posting on Twitter/X, but not me.

I try to post at least two to three times a week. It seems to sell books, but even if it doesn't, it's fun, and while it was foreign to me at the beginning, it's now within my comfort zone.

Podcasts: I've been on over twenty-five podcasts talking about my books, my career pivot from attorney to writer, my life . . . whatever the interviewer would like to discuss.

These days, I've become a little more selective about which podcast I'll appear on and have some criteria. I like podcasts where the interviewer has read one or more of my books and has some idea about my background and career path. Sometimes, the interviewer has read none of the book and starts down a line of questions that have nothing to do with me or the book.

I like podcasters who ask me questions and have conversations with me. I'm there to talk, but some don't have a conversation and don't conduct an interview. These podcasters use their show as a forum to do most of the talking. It's their show, but it's not a productive or fun experience for me.

I try to stay far away from podcasters who rant. Ranting doesn't sell the kinds of books I write. I try to stay away from podcasters who want to have a substantive discussion about bankruptcy law or any law for that matter. I'm retired. I'm not giving out advice anymore and even if I was, I wouldn't give it on a podcast. I save my bankruptcy law discussions these days for my still-practicing-bankruptcy-attorney friends.

I use a podcast pitch to get myself in front of the show hosts. It takes research and time to figure out how to get in front of a podcaster for the pitch.

Well within my comfort zone.

Advertising: Here's a topic for which my liberal arts background has provided me with no training at all. I'm one hundred percent trial and error on this one. So far, I've experienced more error than trial.

I've tried Amazon ads. They were pricey. They sold books and delivered Kindle Unlimited pages read, but I never did much better than break even. For those who don't know, Amazon ads are an auction of space where your ad will appear. For me, I hoped my ad would appear in two different places: landing pages like Michael Connelly's or John Grisham's books, down below where Amazon shows other books under the heading "You May Also Like," and at the end of a Kindle book with the same prompt. The advertising author pays by the click. If a potential buyer clicks on the ad, they're redirected to the advertised Amazon book landing page for the potential buyer to learn more. The author pays for the click whether or not there's a sale. Amazon auctions ad space off in real time. The author has to decide how much they're willing to pay for the space. Amazon provides a range of bid prices. You can imagine that a bid of just one dollar quickly becomes quite expensive if there are hundreds of clicks a day but only a few sales.

I now use Facebook ads more and more; the auction concept is like Amazon's auction, but Facebook seems to cost less than Amazon and seems to reach more potential book buyers by allowing me to define the audience who'll see the ad in their feed by age, gender, location, and interests. I can try out different combinations of audience demographics to see what works and who's reading the books. I typically post an image related to the book with some words geared toward a very short, to-the-point advertisement and then "boost" the post. So far, it's been working.

Online advertising is a complicated and layered topic. I'm still trying to learn the advertising techniques and options, algorithms, audiences, and more. It's not quite in my comfort zone yet, but I plod on.

Contests: I enter each of my books in about ten contests. Contest wins provide credibility and cred sells books. A gold medal here and a silver medal there help and I can post about a win on social media. There are lots of legitimate contests to try: Reader's Favorite, Reader Views, and Literary Titan, to name a few.

Book Trailers: I like to have a service produce a one minute mini-movie for each book. It's fun to oversee the project, not expensive, and it gives me something else I can post about on social media. It's also rewarding to see an overview of my book come alive, and it allows me to wonder if a Hollywood movie of my book would look something like the trailer, if Hollywood ever picked up the book and made a movie of it.

After the last trailer for *Cram Down*, I was thinking Kerry Washington would play the part of 3J.

Hey, a boy can dream, right?

Reviews: Positive reviews sell books. Fifty or more reviews is my goal to show potential buyers that many people have read and reviewed the book.

While I have sufficient reviews for each book, the percentage of readers who read my books and then leave a review is lower than I'd like. Maybe they're being kind because they hated the book and didn't want to write anything negative. Mostly, I don't believe that's what's going on, although, like any writer, I worry about readers who don't like a book. I've come to believe people are uncomfortable leaving a review on Amazon or Goodreads or Barnes & Noble, don't want to bother, or don't want to invest the time.

As a result, the read-to-review ratio is not what I would like to see.

That's unfortunate because reviews are one of the best and most efficient ways to market a book. I'm happy they bought the book. I'm thrilled they read it. I'd be ecstatic if they'd leave a review or even just check the appropriate number of stars.

∽

I'm still learning. Plugging away. Having fun with it. Exploring and growing my comfort zone. Trying to take my liberal arts BA in American Studies and, forty-seven years later, turn it into a minor in marketing earned at the Indie Author's Hard Knocks University.

My call to action for you: if you're a reader and rarely leave reviews, consider at least checking some stars after you've finished a book.

If you do, you'll make an indie author real happy :)

17

You've Published—Congrats!!—Now You're Reading the Reviews. Why?

Now that I'm many books into this writing gig, I've read many of the posted reviews. Should I? Do all authors read them? I'm not sure on both counts. But I read them. Not just the ones on Amazon but also Barnes & Noble, Goodreads, and other online places readers leave reviews.

A "review" is supposed to be "a critical evaluation," according to Merriam-Webster. But not all of them are. Some offer nothing but mean-spirited comments. We writers know this. Sometimes, we learn it in the school of hard knocks. Or perhaps the writing school of hard-knock reviews.

Some people think my books are worthy of five-stars. But I acknowledge the books may not be for everyone, and when my books aren't their cup of tea, maybe the books deserve harsher reviews. But it's also true that the book world is just more and more full of zingers posted by the mean-spirited.

My thesis is simple: most mean-spirited zingers are not the same as reviews. They are anything but critical evaluations.

In writing this piece about reviews, I'm guided by Isaac Asimov's insightful observation: "From my close observation of writers . . . they fall into two groups: 1) those who bleed copiously and *visibly* at any bad review, and 2) those who bleed copiously and *secretly* at any bad review."

I'm also influenced by a comment Diane Lane made when describing the need to have a Teflon soul: "Either cook with it or let it slide." This is my moment to cook with it and talk about reviews. After this, I'll dip myself in some Teflon and hope forever to let it slide.

So states the writer's lament.

෴

I should start by reporting I'm used to criticism.

Wait. You smirked. I saw it. You thought, "Yeah, right." You whispered, "Is anyone *used to* criticism?" I heard you.

No . . . really, I am. It doesn't bother me. Well, it mostly doesn't bother me.

Here's the cold hard truth: any attorney who works at a large firm gets used to criticism. From the boss. From the chair of your practice group. From the managing partner. From your colleagues. From the associates who work for you. From a judge. From opposing counsel. From the United States Trustee. From the client. From your administrative assistant. From the staff. It happens.

If you're going to survive in the firm and the practice, the sooner you get a thick skin, the sooner you'll open the door to a successful career.

But even with a professional lifetime of criticism under my belt, nothing quite prepared me for the book review process and the pain it can bring.

So, as Isaac observed, I've bled. Sometimes visibly and sometimes secretly, but it's actual blood. Copious red drops of it on the floor by the desk where I live my new life of writing. A trail of blood leading from the Amazon and Goodreads review pages to my keyboard and my next book and my next.

I'm here to report that absorbing reviews from the public has been a fascinating experience. Most of the reviews are thoughtful, well-written, and honest. Fair, critical evaluations. Just like the Merriam-Webster definition of "reviews" requires.

To each of those reviewers, I offer a heartfelt "thanks," regardless of whether your review was positive or negative and whether you gave me two stars or five.

To those reviewers, I say that you read the book and took the time to let the rest of the world know how you felt about it. Bravo! It only takes a moment to leave a review, but I know it's a moment out of your life, and I just want you to know that your review means a lot to me.

There are, however, some doozy reviews posted for each of my books that sometimes make me grimace. As Taylor Swift said, "Nothing ruins your day more than getting a bad review." More than once, these doozy reviews have turned a sunny day stormy and left my head itchy and in need of a scratch.

Here are some examples.

Someone left a one-star review because he didn't like the title of one of my books: *Unfair Discrimination*. The actual review was this: "Silly title, as apposed [sic] to FAIR Discrimination?" I'm mostly sure he didn't actually read the book to understand why it was so titled, but I'll get to that in a second.

Now, I don't want to be nitpicky and I certainly don't want to review a reviewer's words, but the use of "apposed" is incorrect grammar. The proper word to have used in leaving this stinging comment would have been "opposed." There are lots of grammar articles on the internet to help a writer learn whether to use apposed or opposed. Here's one: *https://grammarhow.com/apposed-vs-opposed/*.

So the grammatically correct comment should have read: "Silly title, as *opposed* to FAIR Discrimination?"

I'm afraid I must give this reviewer an "F" for his poor grammar. I mean, if you're going to write an uncomplimentary review of an otherwise award-winning book, shouldn't you at least spend a moment or two and get your grammar right? It might even add some gravitas to the review.

More importantly, this reviewer didn't write a critical piece about the book at all. All he did was try to be biting and to criticize, and he didn't even do it well.

Back to the title. "Unfair Discrimination" is a phrase in the bankruptcy code. All of my 3J titles come from a bankruptcy code phrase or concept. Therefore, the title "Unfair Discrimination" is not at all silly. It's the federal law of the land and a very important part of the Chapter 11 reorganization process. If you're truly interested in this matter, look at 11 U.S.C. § 1129(b)(1).

I taught bankruptcy law for many years and when we got to this part of the bankruptcy code, I would tell the students that all discrimination in the world is unfair *except* in bankruptcy, where the law deems that some forms of discrimination are fair.

If he had read the book, it would have been easy to understand why the title was à propos—early on, the book informs the reader of the significance of the phrase and its importance to the storyline.

But the big "if" in the prior sentence is important. He only read the title. Not the book. And it leads me to the following concern (because I'm confident this reviewer didn't read the book): should Amazon and Goodreads allow a person to review a book he didn't read?

. . . Deep cleansing breath . . .

Another reviewer complained about a book containing off-colored language. Swear words. She doesn't like books like that and said that was a "hard stop" for her. She thanked me for giving her a free book. So, it's proper for me to say, "You're welcome," and it would be sensible for me to try not to dwell on the review.

But in this chapter, dwelling is my thing and I'm bothered by the free book issue. Is the moral for me "You get what you are paid for?" For sure. Here, she paid nothing, and I got nothing other than an unsolicited public warning that my book had some adult language in it.

I mean, what is she? The town crier letting the reading world know the book has some swear words in it?

But I'm more bothered by the review, so here are some facts. The book she read contained authentic dialogue in accordance with my goal when I write a legal thriller. I want it to reflect what actually happens between attorneys behind the scenes and between lenders and borrowers at the negotiating table. Truth be told, in some of those real-life interactions, people swear, including the attorneys, the bankers, and the borrowers. They get angry. The 3J series reflects those real life interactions.

In my books, people swear. Because, in my life, people swear.

This was another example of a reviewer failing to leave a "review." Nothing critical at all. No evaluation. Perhaps I should have included in the free giveaway some form of rating ("R") or warning of my own that the book contained "adult language."

My bad. Maybe I will the next time I do a giveaway.

She also gave the book a two-star rating and, therefore, I have another question. Since what she wrote was a warning, not a review, why did she check stars and why only two? Why did she even have the option to check stars?

I would suggest that contrary to what a two-star designation suggests, I did a great job with my cuss words, and since I know cuss words better than she does, I can assure you these were outstanding five-star cuss words.

I respect that the reviewer didn't like this kind of book, but it's also important to note that there were cuss words in the first chapter. I suspect her "hard stop" comment meant she didn't read past the first chapter because that was as far as she needed to go if she didn't like cuss words.

The question is the same as above: should people review books they didn't read?

Again, a deep, cleansing breath . . .

Lastly, one reviewer wanted me to write sex scenes in my thrillers. A fair, albeit prurient, desire, I suppose, in an unfair, perhaps prurient world. But is it a fair expectation that there will be explicit sex scenes in a legal thriller? Maybe the reviewer should find an explicit romance genre novel next time for any needed dose of unrealistic, yet multi-orgasmic, sex? You know, the novels with mostly naked, buff lovers on the cover.

Just wondering.

Okay. Three rants to get my point across. Very sorry. Now, hundreds of reviews into my writing career, I've finally begun to learn something Nicholas Cage said: "You can't make your choices based on what critics think. You have to make your choices based on what's honest for you."

So, even as I rant a bit about reviews, what's honest for me is that reviews are here to stay. I'll just have to learn to take the good with the bad and be my honest self.

But here's the thing: it's not only me. We live in a written review/number of stars world. We live in a time when people have lost track of the difference between being critical and just criticizing. There is a difference. Really, there is.

This applies not just to books. But to everything. The review and star world created by Amazon and other onliners certainly worried me as I began my book-writing journey. How would readers react? How brutal would their comments be?

For comparison, as I got into the writing gig and tried to appreciate the review process, I wondered what readers were saying about books written by famous bestselling authors.

I read some of those bestseller reviews. It was an eye-opening experience.

What Makes Me ... Me

Turns out it's not just indie authors who draw the ire of reviewers. For example, even Michael Connelly gets some humdinger reviews.

Connelly's a brilliant writer and an impressive speaker. One of my favorite authors. When he speaks, he talks about his writing style and how he gets ideas for books. That's engaging, but I'd love to hear him speak about reviews. I'd like to hear his feelings about the humdingers. I'd love for him to take up the cause and compel Amazon to require reviewers to read the books they want to review.

I'd love for him to help us indie authors out and promote civility. I realize that civility doesn't sell his books, but it might sell mine and it would preserve our mental health, an important cause in the world we live in—especially for indie authors like me.

18

Just My Two Cents—Filtered

I'M NO LONGER a "what you see is what you get" guy. I'm filtered these days. It takes a little work. It takes a little time. But I highly recommend filtering.

In my early days, I was a guy with viewpoints. My head was full of them. Sometimes, covering lots of topics. Back then, I had little use for a filter. If I thought it, I wrote it down and sent it out. Since I thought a lot, I wrote a lot. My Two Cents—Unfiltered.

Some of it was offensive to some. Some not.

At first, I didn't care who in my audience of readers I offended. But it turns out that's not the greatest way to go through life. Eventually, I wondered, who had given me a license to offend people? No one, of course. I had no such license. No one does.

Luckily, by the time I had figured it out, I had only offended several dozen people (well, maybe more) before I started cultivating some filters.

I now use the filters for all of my written communications. Well . . . 99.5% of them.

Maybe filters are one of the few things you gain, instead of lose, with age.

Now that I'm old(er), I'm a firm believer that the one communicating should be the one employing the filter. But in our modern era, all too often, we seem to leave the filter to the reader, not the writer. We tell the reader to have a thick skin. We don't seem to tell the writer to consider how their words can hurt.

That's a shame. The world might be a better place if the people communicating employed a filter or two.

I try to. I keep things simple so I can remember how to filter. These days, I use two filters: the aging process filter and a brief editorial review filter. They work in tandem, something like this.

Aging Filter: Instead of an idea going straight from my brain to the computer (in the old days, the typewriter) and then out for publication and into the public, the idea first goes through the aging filter and sits for a while. Setting it aside and then revisiting it a little while later. Nothing better than processing what I was going to say before saying it. Like some wine. Let my "idea tannins" age a little and mellow in that aging process.

The idea might get better with a bit of aging. Or my idea might sour and turn to vinegar. If it does, I throw it out and start over with another idea. Either way, it will most definitely benefit from a little time in the filter. If the idea doesn't do well in the aging filter, no worries. The world didn't need to hear the idea, anyway.

Editorial Review Filter: "Writing without revising is the literary equivalent of waltzing daily out of the house in your underwear." – *Patricia Fuller*. Going live with an idea without giving it a chance for revision might be the equivalent of waltzing out of the house completely naked. That might be okay for some. Not for others. With my unfiltered words, I waltzed out naked many times in my youth, but at this point in my life, clothing is critical. I'm confident the world doesn't need to see a sixty-eight-year-old parading around Denver in the raw. I'm sure my neighbors appreciate I remain clothed. It's also good for me to take some time to contemplate whether I should change and edit and only then publish the thought.

My filters aren't too hard to employ, and they'd work just wonderfully for everyone who has lots of thoughts and wants to offer all of them to the world as their two cents.

But here's the problem I see. There's a good deal of unfiltered notions written and published these days, often as emails or Facebook or "X" posts penned in the heat of the moment. The author writes it and hits the "send" key or "publish" button. Simple.

Instantly, off to the world goes the unfiltered hypothesis. It's as if the writer is saying: "Here's everything. Read what you wish." The only way for the reader to know what to consume is to read everything or nothing. Yuck.

For instance, take politicians. They write a lot. The trouble is, not all of them use any filter at all. You know them. If you still consume news, you see it in your news feed 24/7. Cringeworthy reports popping up on your mobile phone, tablet, and computer. The more cringe, the more newsworthy.

Here's the thing. The world doesn't need to know every notion, good and bad, of every person, including politicians, every minute of every day. No one could have that many thoughts worthy of publishing, and many of those unfiltered ideas do nothing more than parade the communicator around *au naturel* for all the world to see and laugh at. A laugh of derision.

But the trouble is, not everyone laughs. Many instead applaud.

I'm too old to figure out how it got this way; how filtering is now left in the hands of the reader, not the writer. Bass-ackwards if you ask me, but I don't blame Facebook or generic social media or the inventor of email. I blame the writers.

Maybe we should have a limit on written communications each day. Or maybe several designated days each week where all writers must use filters. Or maybe a setting in the newsfeed app that would filter out the unfiltered words. It wouldn't eliminate the problem, but it would sure cut down on the unfiltered noise.

Just a thought. Just my two cents—filtered for your consumption.

19

The Struggle to Belong—The Ode of an Outsider

You may wonder why this is in the "On Writing" section of IW3M. Stay with it. It's not a mistake. It should become clear.

FRANK LLOYD WRIGHT said, "No house should ever be on a hill or on anything. It should be of the hill. Belonging to it. Hill and house should live together, each the happier for the other."

Our nature is to live together, each the happier for the other. Whether in the same household, the same neighborhood, the same community, or the same organization.

We don't do well as loners. Even famous loners have extolled the virtues of belonging. Albert Einstein reflected, "Although I am a typical loner in my daily life, my awareness of belonging to the invisible community of those who strive for truth, beauty, and justice has prevented me from feelings of isolation."

Einstein nailed it. Even loners can belong. Without belonging, there will be isolation. But I'm not much of a belonger.

❧

The pertinent childhood stats: seven homes in twelve years; five grade and middle schools; two high schools. The pertinent life stats: seven states; thirteen cities; twenty-one different addresses.

What happens when you move around so much as a kid? There are consequences. There's a sense of separateness. A sense of being apart from others and other things. A lack of community. An absence of knowing how to be a part of a community. A lack of joining and signing up. A fear of rejection after joining. As a result, a lack of any interest in being part of a community.

A lifelong struggle to belong.

❧

There are other consequences. Habitat for Humanity (and others) recognized that kids who move from house to house, neighborhood to neighborhood, and school to school end up dropping out of school. They don't belong; they see no point, and often, they fill the hole of a lack of belonging by turning to drugs and joining gangs.

They move for economic reasons—the parents can't afford to stay in one rental, so every year or two, they move. Terrible for the integrity of the family. Even worse for the kids' development.

As Habitat says, if you want to solve the gang problems, solve the housing problems. If you want to solve the education problems, solve the housing problems. If you want to solve the drug problems, solve the housing problems.

And we can solve so many more problems by putting families into a house *and having them stay there*. The Habitat dream.

❧

I was lucky. I didn't fill the hole with gangs and drugs. And I got my education.

But I don't belong easily or even well. I learned how to move on, and I made it so. I learned the art of leaving, and I did. I learned to expect friends would fade away, and they did.

I study my lack of belonging from time to time and what I've learned over the decades is that I'm not comfortable with not belonging. It's not something I've gotten used to. It's not something I want. It's not even something I accept. I want to belong. At times, I long to belong. But even as I finish up my seventh decade, I don't always know how to belong. My instinct is to shy away from it.

We all gravitate to the things with which we are comfortable and the things we know how to do. I do. I know how to be an outsider.

I'm no longer a drifter or a transient and haven't been since I grew up and left home (or whatever home it was at the time I left). I'm just not a belonger.

I've learned something else about not being a belonger. I can be crabby. I'm hard to be around. I'm not the comic book scientist who was exposed to radiation and now has a green monster inside into which he transforms. I've just learned that when you're crabby, not only is it hard to belong, but not many people want you to belong. Not to them. Not in their world.

Not belonging is a self-fulfilling prophecy. I don't belong, and with some exceptions, no one wants me to, either.

I marvel at those with "networks." Their friends, family, acquaintances. I have friends, but I'm not good at staying in touch. I have a family—same. I have acquaintances, but I worry that when they see me, they'll bluntly ask, "Who are you?" I guess they're plainly not acquaintances if they don't remember who I am.

Which, in a roundabout way, brings me to writing and why this chapter is in the writing section of this book.

One reason I like to write is I don't have to belong to anything in order to write. It's just me. My club of one. My MacBook and me and the internet and my books for research. I don't have to involve others. It's an endeavor of one. My own solo flight.

I worry, however, that by writing, I've given up whatever fight I have left in me to learn how to belong. But maybe not. When I've written a book and people read it and talk to me about the book—the story, the characters, the plot—suddenly, I belong.

To what? To a group that's interested in what I've done. Curious about what I've created. Communicating with me about . . . me and mine. I belong to the discussion. I belong to the story. Sometimes, I am the story. I belong to the process. It's not quite Einstein's truth, beauty, and justice, but it's something, and it does a great job of fending off feelings of isolation.

When you've spent your life on the outside, even something as small as belonging to a process you've created is huge. So even as writing is isolating and a solitary endeavor, maybe I find writing so important because, for the first time in many, many long years, I belong. I create and wait for others to reach out to me.

My own little club of my own doing, but a club, nonetheless.

Maybe next up, I'll join a community center. But not right away. No point in getting carried away and rushing things.

Ice & Snow

20

The Attempted Assault, Battery & Theft—Much Ado About Nuthin'

I'M A HOCKEY fan. I've never skated well. I fall a lot and can't turn. Not on a dime. Not on a hundred-dollar bill. So, instead of participating, I've always watched. My dad was a fan as well. His friend John, too.

New Haven was a hockey town. The New Haven Blades was an Eastern Hockey League club that skated in New Haven from 1954 to 1972. The Blades played their home games at the New Haven Arena, near the corner of Grove and Orange Streets, demolished in 1974 to make way for an FBI building.

If you like hockey, you know a low wall surrounds the ice, on top of which are glass sheets through which the fans can watch the game. At some point, it was tempered glass. Since 2018, it's been sheets of something called "hockey glass," lab-created safety polycarbonate plexiglass. The sheets are durable, flexing to absorb the shock of the puck and players crashing into them. They encircle the entire arena, including the space behind the players' benches.

They keep the fans safe from the puck and the fans away from the players.

The New Haven Arena, circa 1968, however, had no glass, tempered or otherwise. The rink had a low wall on which sat a chain link fence that didn't go around the entire rink. No fence behind the benches. The fence didn't absorb the puck or the players, and it didn't keep the fans away from the players.

Like so many minor league hockey fans, the Blades' faithful drank to excess and then headed into the blue-collar arena for a night of minor league hockey.

*

To give you a sense of minor league hockey, fans aren't always there to see the home team win or to see a good, competitive game. While both are nice when they happen, the fans are there, liquored up, to see fighting on the ice. I remember one minor league game I saw on a road trip to Spokane, Washington with my wife and son. Friday night, minor league hockey in America. We sat next to an older, gray-haired gentleman who sat with his arms crossed. Silent. He seemed like a proper student of the game.

Ten minutes into the first period, however, with the score 0-0, he stood up animated, cupped his hands around his mouth, and yelled—like a foghorn—admonishing the hometown team and advising them of his disappointment: "I don't see any blood yet, you pussies!" The surrounding fans cheered. A fight broke out in due time. I'm not sure if it had anything to do with his colorful commentary. But that's pretty much minor league hockey for you in a nutshell.

*

Back to New Haven and the Blades.

One Friday night, my dad and John took me to a game. I can't recall who the Blades played that night. But near the end of the second period, a huge fight broke out on the ice. We sat a few rows behind the visiting team's bench.

What Makes Me . . . Me

The visiting players had no separation from the fans because whoever had designed the Arena installed no chain-link fence behind the bench. The benches cleared, and the fight consumed more and more players from each team. With no one watching the visitor's bench, John rose, walked down to the bench, and pilfered the goalie's gloves. Just like that.

As he did, the hometown fans who saw him roared their approval. That swell of emotion caught the visiting goalie's attention, and he looked away from the Blades player he was trying to pummel to figure out what was going on. He saw John making off with the expensive goalie gloves, screamed out something vulgar, and skated back to the bench. With his skates on, he slowly hopped over the short wall behind the bench and gingerly walked into the stands, balancing on his blades as he went. His destination: right for John.

My dad, considerably larger than John and not one to shy away from a confrontation, stepped between the goalie and John.

The goalie stood there, eyeing my dad. Wearing all the goalie gear to protect him from the pain of stopping a hard, frozen rubber puck going ninety miles per hour, he decided my dad couldn't harm him, and wobbling along on his blades, approached my dad. They began pushing and shoving just like everyone else who was duking it out on the ice. My dad's strategy was to push the goalie over when he lost his balance. But it never happened. In seconds, two cops—New Haven's finest that night—came over and separated John, my dad, and the goalie.

So far, so good.

Then, one cop decided to arrest John and my dad and started to try to arrest the goalie as well. John protested, even as he still clutched the stolen gloves.

More cheering. Very loud cheering. More and more fans turned their attention from the fights on the ice to the dispute in the stands.

The second cop pulled my dad and said something, a calm came over my dad, and then the cop and my dad walked out of the stands to the vestibule area. John dropped the gloves, then the first cop let him go and John returned to his seat.

The fans were egging the cop on, yelling that he should arrest the goalie. The remaining cop turned to the goalie as if to arrest him, but the goalie had retrieved his gloves, put them on, and, as he distributed a healthy dose of F-bombs to the Blades' faithful, made his way toward the bench.

The fans encouraged the cop to grab the goalie. But anyone close to the action could see it would've been hard for the cop to put handcuffs on the goalie over the gloves. During a moment of indecision as the cop tried to figure out what his next move would be, the goalie reached the bench and then continued to the ice, and the cop left the scene.

The fights on the ice continued, and the fans returned to cheering and jeering the action on the ice. Some fans made their way down to the fence, reached over, and pummeled the visiting team's players. The players punched back.

Friday night hockey anarchy. Just another chapter in my hockey education.

But where was my dad?

The referees got the situation on the ice under control and doled out major fighting penalties. When the penalized players cleared the ice, it was only a game of three-on-three, plus the goalies. Before any further meaningful skating occurred, the period ended.

Still no dad.

Usually, we walked around in the vestibule in the twenty-minute intermission between periods, checking out the faithful and maybe grabbing a Coke. Coke was our tradition. This time, we didn't move from our seats. John just sat there next to me during the break, saying nothing. Maybe he was thanking his lucky stars that he wouldn't have to call his wife to bail him out of jail or come see him in the hospital. Maybe he was worried that if he had to call her, she wouldn't come. Maybe he wished he hadn't dropped the gloves, although for the life of me, I don't know what he wanted with them.

What Makes Me ... Me

He certainly would not get the visiting goalie to autograph them, and his hockey-playing days had long ago ended.

My dad still had not returned when the third period began. Ten minutes into the third period, he came back with a Coke. "Here. Drink this," he said to me, possibly in an effort to continue our tradition, albeit not during intermission. I drank the Coke. He was, after all, my dad and a tradition was a tradition.

"What happened out there?" John asked.

My dad stared at the action on the ice, shook his head, and said, "Nuthin' happened."

"Did you get me a Coke, too?" John asked.

"Like I said. Nuthin' happened."

End of discussion.

We left a few minutes before the game ended. I don't remember if the Blades won or not. I never found out what happened. Maybe the cop and my dad were acquaintances and had a beer or a Coke together and laughed.

I don't know if the *New Haven Register* reported about the game, the fight on the ice, or the altercation in the stands.

Maybe the newspaper looked at it the same way my dad had reported it: "Nuthin' happened." Not newsworthy without an arrest in the vestibule or in the stands.

I tried to explain all of this the next morning to friends at school before the first class bell sounded. It seemed like a story everyone would gather around to hear in homeroom period. But since I didn't know if anything had happened between the cop and my dad, and if so, what had happened, it was a story without a conclusion and not one that kept my audience engaged.

I wished John had kept the goalie gloves. Then he could have loaned them to me, and I could have brought them to school. That would have kept the audience engaged.

Instead, sometimes life and hockey fights are as Shakespeare observed: they're "Much Ado About Nuthin'."

21

Tobogganing & Long-Term Relationships

It snowed a lot when I was a teenager. Nothing was more fun and exciting than going with my younger brother, David, to a part of the Yale University grounds in the Westville part of New Haven, Connecticut, and riding our toboggans down the long, rolling hills.

A toboggan is a long, flat-bottomed, runnerless sled made of wood slats that curve up and form a cursive "C" shape at the front. They're usually about eighteen inches wide and four to nine feet long. Ours had ropes along the sides that we could grab for stability as we rode.

While a rider can lean to maneuver the toboggan, lift the front, or drag their feet in the snow to steer, mostly, it's a one-directional vehicle—straight ahead only. So, the best place to ride a toboggan was a straight downhill run in fresh snow.

According to the Encyclopedia Britannica, the runnerless toboggan was a native North American invention. The word "toboggan" comes from the Mi'kmaq word *tobakun*, which means sled. In fact, the Inuit made the first toboggans out of whalebone and used them to transport people and belongings across the snowy tundra.

Each winter after I turned sixteen, we'd wait for a snowfall of four inches or more, hoping for the powdery, lightweight kind, not a wet snowfall that would slow down our rides. When we got a powdery fall, with my newly minted Connecticut driver's license, we'd put out toboggans into the back seat, drive in the family's Ford Pinto toward West Haven and get as close as we could to the wooded trailhead that led to the pristine snow-covered hills.

We'd sneak through a part of the chain-link fence that someone had cut so we could trespass on Yale's private land and carry our toboggans a quarter of a mile on the trail to the clearing at the top of a grand hill. There, we'd sit on our toboggans and lurch back and forth, inching them forward.

Once the toboggans began their descent, they picked up speed, and within moments, we were racing down the hill, going what seemed like fifty miles per hour or more. At the end of the run, the toboggans came to rest at the bottom of the hill.

We dusted the snow off and trudged up the hill, toboggans dragging behind us for the next ride and the next toboggan high. It was cold and windy, but we didn't notice.

It was one of those kid things I've never forgotten. New Haven, Connecticut, was a former industrial town that had seen hard times, but riding down the Yale hills after a snowstorm made New Haven seem special.

~§~

I met Loren, my wife of over forty-five years, when I was a junior in college. She lived in Western Kansas, so that first Thanksgiving in 1975 after we met, I invited her home to Connecticut to spend the holiday with my family.

I had just turned twenty, and I was in the first days of the beginning of my adulthood. But I didn't feel like an adult. I was still a teenager, as far as I was concerned.

A day or two after we arrived home from college, it snowed. Powder. Over four inches. Perfect to feed the tobogganing habit.

What Makes Me . . . Me

She had never tobogganed. Not too many suitable hills on the High Plains in Western Kansas to sustain a love for tobogganing.

When the snow let up, I invited her to come with David and me and ride her first toboggan. She was a cautious person but was game. In retrospect, there's no question she agreed out of ignorance. Had she known what was in store, I'm confident she would have declined the invitation.

David sat in the back of the Pinto, squished in with our two toboggans and off we went from Alston Avenue to Edgewood Avenue, then to Forest Road, past the Hopkins Day School, and finally to the fence and the secret entrance to the Yale hills.

She hiked with us to the crest of our favorite hill. The original plan was to have her sit in the front of the longer toboggan and I would ride down with her, sitting just behind her.

We positioned the long toboggan and gave her a quick lesson on how things worked. She got on, tucked her legs under the front curl, and grabbed the ropes on either side of the toboggan. I sat behind with my legs on either side of her. We rocked back and forth and the toboggan inched forward.

After a few seconds of rocking, however, I rolled off the toboggan and gave her a push in the back, just enough to send the toboggan and her on her maiden voyage streaking down the hill.

I'm not sure why I hopped off and let her ride down alone. A spur-of-the-moment decision.

Maybe I figured the quick lesson was all she needed. Maybe I was feeling devilish. Maybe I should have asked how she felt about riding down alone.

Maybe I was still feeling the tug of my former teenage years.

Turns out she was a natural at riding it fast. But it also turns out the decision to hop off was not my best moment, and she screamed the entire way down.

Just twenty seconds of a ride, but I'm sure it was terrifying. She may have even gone airborne as she rode up and over a large snowdrift. I hopped on the back of David's toboggan and we rode down together to congratulate her on her first ride. No broken bones. No bruises. A complete success.

But that's not how she viewed it at the moment. She was having no part in any celebration. Powdered snow covered her face, chest, and arms, and she was madder than hell. Instantly, I was worried. It was such a stupid idea to roll off and let her fly down the hill alone.

Because of my decision, I wondered if the continuation of our relationship was in doubt. I figured that was the end of our time together. I worried the next thing I heard would be that she wanted a ride to the Amtrak train station near downtown and would head back to Bryn Mawr, Pennsylvania, without me, to hunker down in her dormitory alone for the holiday, maybe eating a soggy packaged turkey sandwich from *Wawa* on Thanksgiving.

But none of that happened. Much to my surprise, she wanted to ride again.

We grabbed the toboggan and hauled it back up the hill for her second ride. She was hooked. The only difference on this next ride: she sat in the back. Where she could keep an eye on me. We rode together, both screaming, this time with joy, not fear.

Easy to understand. Another toboggan addict.

Later that winter, back at college, we found an old sled, and after a weekend snowstorm, rode down the hill behind Haverford College's Barclay dorm to the duck pond below. Not a toboggan, but it turns out she loved any ride down a snowy hill.

When you're sixty, going down a snow-covered hill at breakneck speed can make you feel young all over again . . . and when you're twenty, if you're lucky, it may even be good for a long-term relationship.

22

"Kill Him!!!"—The Case of the New England Whalers Game Incident

1976. HOME FOR a break with my girlfriend, Loren (the same one who learned to toboggan the hard way with me over the past Christmas break).

We had two major items on the agenda. First, I had two of my wisdom teeth extracted.

Then, the next day, we drove up to Hartford to see the New England Whalers hockey team play.

The Whalers played in the World Hockey Association in the Hartford Civic Center. Later, teams in the WHA would merge into the National Hockey League, including the Whalers, who then changed their name to the Hartford Whalers (because the Boston Bruins objected to a team claiming all of New England as their own) until the team moved to North Carolina.

My dad had somehow scored first-row seats between the center red line and a blue line, right up at the glass. Translation: we sat near center ice right up front and could stand and pound the glass with our hands to cheer on the Whalers.

Loren wasn't a hockey fan. Her maiden voyage down the Yale hills in a toboggan was pretty close to her fill of winter sports. But she was game, and we drove up from New Haven for forty-five minutes to see the action and introduce her to the game.

On the way up, she warned me she didn't enjoy fighting and would be upset if a fight broke out in the game.

Hmm. Her expectation of professional hockey without the occasional glove-dropping fight on the ice was . . . well, quite unrealistic. Isn't that part of what makes hockey the beloved sport that it is?

We arrived at the Civic Center, parked, entered, and found our seats. On the drive up, I had planned to buy her a Whalers jersey, the iconic picture of a whale's fin sticking up out of a "W" icon. By the way, if you look at a map, you'll see that Hartford is nowhere near the water. But the name and the logo had caught on among the Whaler loyalists.

Hockey is a three-period sport. As I recall, it was 2–2 after two periods; the skating was crisp, the checking vigorous, and most importantly for my relationship, there had been no fights. During the intermission, we headed out to the concourse, along with many of the fans. Always a fun time at a hockey game to wander around the arena and check out the crowd.

But the tender gums where my wisdom teeth had been were swelling, and the pain was growing. I just hoped I could make it through the third period and then the drive back to New Haven to put ice on my cheeks. Hockey players get their teeth knocked out all the time and just play through the pain. I just needed to be hockey-tough.

I didn't want to leave. I didn't want to suggest to Loren that she had seen enough. If I had, I would have been able to fulfill her desire to see fightless hockey.

But trooper that I was, I toughed it out, and we returned to our great seats for period three.

Right after the third period began, a huge fight broke out in front of us. A Whaler had checked someone on the visiting team hard into the glass. A nose met the glass not a foot from Loren's nose on the other side of the glass.

Other visiting team members took exception and went after the Whaler. Several Whalers came to the aid of their teammate, and a multi-player fight broke out. For a short while, the referees let the boys be boys and didn't intervene.

All of this was the unfortunate event I had hoped we might avoid when Loren told me she wanted to see no fights at the Civic Center that night.

Between my concern over Loren's expected reaction and the pain in my swelling cheeks, I slumped down in my seat and hoped for the best. What else could I do?

In seconds, however, out of the corner of my eye, I saw Loren rise, lean over to the glass, pound it with both fists, and yell, "Kill Him!!!!" at full volume. The fan sitting next to her approved and cheered her reaction.

⋘

We drove home that night in silence. As we approached our exit off of I-91, I asked, "So you enjoyed yourself?"

"It was great. That fight wasn't so bad after all."

"Not so bad? Hmm. Seemed like you really liked it."

She smiled. "I don't like fights."

"But I'm guessing you liked hockey."

"I liked hockey, indeed."

⋘

My mouth healed, memories of the Whaler's fight faded, and years later, we now live in Denver.

Together, we watch the Colorado Avalanche, Denver's NHL franchise, on television and sometimes in person. The Quebec Nordiques, a former World Hockey Association team, just like the Whalers, moved to Denver in May 1995 and became the Avalanche.

So, in a very roundabout way, Loren's love for hockey, brought on that night at her first and only WHA game, and her first, but not only, hockey fight, continues here in Denver as she watches and loves a team with WHA roots.

She'd never admit it, but she's grown to like not only the best skaters in the world, but some of the best brawlers as well.

And there's something about standing up for yourself that makes hockey fights so purposeful.

Pop Culture & Me

23

No Satisfaction & What You Want & Need—My Request to Mick and Keith

Two of my favorite Rolling Stones songs are "(I Can't Get No) Satisfaction" and "You Can't Always Get What You Want," both written by Mick Jagger and Keith Richards. Both songs got into my head at an early age and have stayed there ever since. Here's a little about the songs and why.

The Stones released "Satisfaction" in 1965, and it appeared on the American album version of *Out of Our Heads*. It reached number one on the Billboard Hot 100 List and held that position for four weeks, knocked off the top spot by the Herman's Hermits' "I'm Henry the Eighth, I Am" (am I dating myself or what?). It was thirty-first on *Rolling Stone* magazine's "The 500 Greatest Songs of All Time" list in 2021.

Keith Richards opens the song with one of the most iconic guitar riffs ever played. Experts widely suggest the song is about sexual frustration, and in fact, it only played on pirate radio stations in Britain for a while because the radio powers believed the song was too sexually suggestive. Perhaps, but as you get older and continue to listen to the song, you could attribute any genre of frustration to it.

"You Can't Always Get What You Want" appeared on the Rolling Stones' 1969 album *Let It Bleed*. The song preaches that even if you can't get what you want, you can get what you need. To get it, all you have to do is just try sometime.

In 2004, *Rolling Stone* magazine named the song the hundredth greatest rock and roll song of all time. Personally, I would've placed it much higher on the list. Why? Like "Satisfaction," it speaks to me.

I don't mean to overthink the songs, but in life, satisfaction and needs are powerful goals that drive us as we journey through it all. Both songs have prompted me to weigh whether I'm satisfied if I get what I need, and as I ponder the issue of satisfaction, I wonder if Mick and Keith were right that I could really get it.

∽

I find it interesting, even ironic, that Mick and Keith told us in 1965 how frustrated they were to the point they couldn't get satisfaction, sexual or otherwise. And then told us in 1969 they could get what they needed, even if it wasn't everything they wanted. If I were a therapist, I would conclude that in a scant four years, the boys were experiencing less frustration and had matured into addressing some important life issues.

In their own way. As only a Rolling Stone could.

While they mention frustration in passing in one verse of "You Can't Always Get What You Want," it never resonated with me. I'm sure they were less frustrated by then because, in the years between 1962 and 1969, the Stones went from a London blues band playing bar gigs to one of the greatest rock and roll bands of all time (I would have said the greatest, but I want to give everyone's different tastes their fair due and acknowledge that the Beatles and other legendary bands have a claim to the GOAT title).

They were atop the rock and roll world. So, of course, the

What Makes Me . . . Me

members of the Stones were not mere mortals by 1969. They were the Stones, and as Keith Richards observed: "You have the sun, you have the moon, you have the air that you breathe—and you have the Rolling Stones!"

In 1965's "Satisfaction," Mick sang to us that he was on a losing streak. Then he sang to us in 1969 that a girl with bloody hands was great at deception.

I completely understood the notion of a 1965 losing streak, even though I doubted Mick and Keith were on one. Certainly not after releasing "Satisfaction." But I never understood if that 1969 girl was someone Mick wanted but couldn't have. Or was she someone he needed and could have if he just tried?

But wait a second. This was Mick Jagger singing. He could have any girl he wanted or needed (well, maybe anyone besides Carly Simon. Just listen to "You're So Vain," but that's a topic for another essay someday). And I'm sure he didn't even have to try.

Or maybe it wasn't a Mick-centered lyric at all. Maybe the girl was the issue. Was there something she wanted but couldn't have? Was it Mick she wanted? Remember, he saw her at the gathering. Or was it something she could get because she needed it? Was it Mick she needed and could get?

Did any of it involve deception and blood?

I'm uncertain about the blood, but after all, the Stones titled the album "Let It Bleed." Blood aside, I'm equally uncertain about who wanted and needed what or whom. But it's a wonderful illustration of how complicated this want-versus-need thing is. Thanks, Mick and Keith, for pointing that out.

Like no other band, the Stones could bookend a decade between an absence of satisfaction at one end and not getting everything they wanted at the other end and throw in a little blood, reception, and deception for good measure.

By 1969, the Stones could say stuff like this and, to those of us who listened over and over to the song, drive us to wonder about our own wants and needs.

While the song spoke to me, I've also always wondered how truthful it was. By 1969, the Stones could undoubtedly get everything they needed, and not just sometimes. In fact, I'm certain they could, and did, get anything they wanted as well. By then, for the Stones, the want versus need thing was a non-issue. Potentially very uncomplicated.

For the rest of us, who can't get what we want and sometimes can't get what we need either, we find the want-versus-need thing complicated.

I've never solved the mystery of the lyrics. All I've ever known is this: by 1969, like many teenagers, I had already lived an existence without satisfaction and started to worry that I was well on my way to getting neither what I wanted nor what I needed in life. So, the songs prompted me to consider my wants and needs. Despite not solving the mystery of the song lyrics (and the blood), it nevertheless was inspirational and educational.

Inspirational: If I could just get what I needed in life, how fabulous would that be?

Educational: It spurred me on to wonder what did I really need? The year 1969 was the first time I can remember wondering about that. It wasn't the last.

Mick and Keith should get some of the credit for my life's quest of trying to figure out what I need and how I might get it. But I would also love them to do a reissue of the song (I'm sure they'll put that on their to-do list as soon as they read this) with less blood and more insight and address, and perhaps clear up, some things:

What do we all need?

- A roof, food, some hope for a better future (in 1969, the end of the war and the draft would have been nice).
- Peace. Love. Friends. Happiness? Of course, but these may be more wants we can't always have, try as we might. Certainly, peace these days seems only an aspiration at best. Sometimes we're lucky and have love, and sometimes not.

Sometimes we have friends for life, and sometimes we move on (or just move away). And happiness can be quite illusory. People live without these four, but there's no question they'd live better with them. I have my doubts about whether we can get these, especially if all we do is just try for them. That's why they seem like wants, not needs, to me.

- What of success? Do we need that? What is it? Its definition is illusive. It's different for different people. If you can't define it, how can you know if you need it, and if you don't know if you need it, how can you figure out how to get it?
- And wants and needs are not static. They change.

Complicated stuff. Maybe not as complicated as the deceptive, bloody girl, but complicated nonetheless.

So if Mick and Keith take me up on my suggestion and reissue the song, they're gonna have their hands full.

˜

There's more about wants and needs that I don't know than I do. But, here's what I know.

Did I ever get everything I needed as time went on? I'm sure I didn't, but I've learned as I've aged that I need (and want) a lot less than I believed I did when I was younger. That's a lucky thing. Because if I live long enough, I expect there will come a time when I need nothing and can't even remember what I want.

When that happens and I check out from this life, I sure wish I'll come back in my next life as Mick. I would have said Mick or Keith, but have you seen Keith in his old age? Coming back as just Mick would be sufficient and the right call.

Yup. Coming back as Mick Jagger might be the one thing that, if I try sometimes, I'll find it's just what I need.

24

Lennon & McCartney

WHEN I INCLUDED a chapter in *IW3M* about Mick Jagger and Keith Richards, it worried me. I wondered that if I wrote my "Request to Mick and Keith," how would I then escape the need to write something about John Lennon and Paul McCartney? And what would the chapter be? What brilliant observations could I possibly offer?

I've read lots of books about Lennon and McCartney. I've seen lots of movies about them. I adore them and always will. Everything I needed to learn in life, I learned from them. Well, almost everything.

So many have written so much about them, and it might be hubris to think I've got something new to say. But I didn't want anyone to assume that was because the duo holds no place in my life. To the contrary. They are so important in my life that I'm left without creative words to write about them.

So, I fretted, *should I write this chapter or not?* On one level, how could I not? These two were my top heroes among many pop heroes. These two changed the world and me along with it. These two inspired me in ways no other pop stars ever have or ever will.

What Makes Me . . . Me

On another level, however, I couldn't write a deep, psychologically analytical piece about their lyrics, their lives, and their relationship with each other and then tie it to my life. If I tried to, I would likely fail. Write a deep analytical chapter? No. I couldn't and shouldn't. Above all else, I wanted to avoid being just another Beatles fan extolling the virtues of . . . well . . . the Beatles.

Maybe I could write about the Beatles' breakup and join a litany of commentators who've addressed the topic, lamenting how sad I felt in 1970 when the breakup announcement hit the newspapers. Was it Paul or John (or George) who killed the Beatles? Did it matter? Wasn't the death of the Beatles sad enough without having to attribute the smoking gun to a particular member of the group?

Breakup concept rejected. They broke up. They were never getting back together again. Life happens. We all move on, whether or not we want to.

Maybe I could write about the recent Peter Jackson documentary *Get Back*, offering us incredible access to the chaotic way Lennon and McCartney wrote and recorded songs together. But after watching *Get Back*, there's nothing else to say. The images weren't worth a thousand words. They were worth all the words. The movie records musical genius for us all to see and grants us all access to the private process in such depth that I have nothing to add.

Then I wondered, should this chapter be blank, with just the title *Lennon & McCartney* followed by blank pages? Now, that would be novel. A chapter about the two most important icons in my life that contained no words. Like one of those pop art pieces at a museum of modern art that's completely white. One that art lovers pause to admire, nod their heads knowingly, and suggest through their attentive observation of the blank painting that the message of emptiness is so deep, it needs no design, no color, and no medium.

Yikes. I never liked those hanging pieces in modern art museums. Intriguing notion, but not me. I've seen those paintings and watched those art lovers, and I just find those paintings (and art lovers) silly.

And what would the message of such a chapter be? Certainly not emptiness. That's not how I feel when I listen to "In My Life" or "Eleanor Rigby."

Then it struck me. I would just write a short, to-the-point, *'nuff said* piece. The only one in the book to show how important Lennon and McCartney are to me.

What's a *'nuff said* piece? One in which the author doesn't try to be smarter, wittier, or more skillful than the subject of the piece. I'm not, never have been, and never will be smarter, wittier, or more skillful than Lennon and McCartney. And I don't want to be. I want them to remain on that pedestal with me below them, looking up to them admiringly for the rest of my life.

A *'nuff said* piece says little to nothing and concludes with a sincere, all-knowing nod of the head with the words *'nuff said*.

Not a blank canvas. One with a short design, a quick message, and using an economy of mediums. So here is my *'nuff said* piece about John and Paul. I wrote this as I nodded and smiled. You should read it as you nod and smile.

John Lennon. Paul McCartney. *'Nuff said*.

25

Vinyl Records Are Back? I'm Sorry. When Did They Leave?

SOMEONE ASKED ME, "What kind of décor do you have in your living room?"

I answered, "Modern Vinyl." Lots of it.

Nine years ago, we downsized from our Fairway, Kansas, ranch house with its many built-in bookcases to our Denver, Colorado, high-rise condominium. In the process, we designed a built-in entertainment unit to occupy one of our new condo living room walls. Its function was to display keepsakes, safeguard our stereo, and house our vinyl record collection.

Records?

Yes, records. Collected by both of us since we were high school kids in Hays, Kansas, and New Haven, Connecticut. Almost a thousand of them.

As reported by Yamaha Music, the modern-day record starts out as pellets of polyvinyl chloride, a widely used synthetic plastic polymer. The machines load the pellets into a hopper on the record press, where they're melted and squeezed into what's often referred to as a "biscuit" — a blob of vinyl shaped like a hockey puck. The biscuits get pressed into side one and side two of the record and then cooled and packaged.

In the early 1980s, the pundits announced the death of the biscuits and the resulting records and flooded the market with compact discs. These CDs gave the masses digitized music. Upon hearing the news, we held no garage sale to get rid of our record collection. We never considered it.

I considered writing Don McLean to ask him to add a new verse to "American Pie" about the death of records, but since I never conceded the death, I never wrote Mr. McLean.

To us, records were more than polymer biscuits pressed, cooled, and then stuffed into cardboard jackets adorned with artwork and liner notes. They were our lives. Our personal history. In many respects, they were who we were because we grew up in the golden age of records. All of that could never die.

We could have sold our copy of the self-titled 1969 Blood Sweat and Tears record containing the band's hit "And When I Die" and replaced it with the newly pressed CD of the same recording.

But what would we have accomplished? An alleged wider sound bandwidth? Maybe. Would that have given us a higher fidelity version of "And When I Die" and allowed us to hear all the nuances of the recording we had been missing with our vinyl version? Some said it would. I'm a hard "no" on that notion. They were wrong.

Had we ditched the record and bought the CD, we would have replaced the warm analog sound of a record delivered by a diamond stylus, along with all its bruises and warts, with the cold, pristine sound of a perfect digital file converted to sound by a CD player.

Cold perfection in a warm, imperfect world? Not for us.

Did we long to replace a large, fragile recording medium that needed care with a small, more sturdy version that needed no care? No. We've always been crazy careful with our records. We clean them. We dote over them. We store them lovingly. We drop and lift the turntable needle meticulously. Cleaning, dropping and lifting weren't chores. They were an integral part of the music. The ritual of playing a record. We didn't look at our records as fragile. Just music in need of love and attention that we were happy to provide.

We didn't need a small Frisbee we could toss across the room and treat harshly and still get serviceable sound. We were just fine with an admittedly more fragile medium that had aged admirably, just as I would hope we would also age admirably as we became more and more fragile.

It also went without saying that we could always read the liner notes and appreciate the album art on a vinyl record. On a CD, all the same art and information was there, but we could barely see the art and couldn't read the notes without a special magnifying glass. Maybe it was just us getting old. But maybe no one could see it. With CDs, we lost the experience of learning about the music as we listened to it.

So, we were keeping the records. Period.

I sketched out a drawing of the condo unit for the designer and measured the required storage in inches. The total number of inches we needed to store all of our vinyl was 121 ½ inches. The designer could divide that into as many unit compartments as she liked. But the measurement was critical. Not 100. Not 150. One hundred twenty-one and a half inches. We had more than 121 ½ inches of stuff, so to ensure space for 121 ½ inches of records, we would need to sacrifice some other things.

Mostly books. I concluded we couldn't keep all our books and all our records.

After the sketch, I explained the 121 ½ inches issue to Loren, and she listened without comment. I may not have emphasized that the records took up most of the inches.

One Saturday, before we moved, while Loren was out of the

house on call, I went to U-Haul and came home with book boxes. I went through all our books, separated out the ones that were autographed by the author, and with heartless precision, I packed up boxes of books to bring to Goodwill.

When Loren got home later in the day, she surveyed the book situation, and that night, quietly returned many of the books to their place on our ranch house bookshelves.

And there it was: books versus records. The 121 ½-inch problem had come to a head. How could we ever resolve it?

We met at the conflict resolution table (the kitchen table) to talk.

"It's just a matter of feet and inches," I explained.

Silence.

"Even if we get rid of all the albums, we still won't have enough room for all the books in the new condo," I continued. "Books are bigger. One book might take up the same amount of room as ten records. Something has to give."

She listened. I suggested that getting rid of books made logical sense because we had Kindles and we could continue to read to our heart's content. We would just have to abandon the more tactile experience of touching the cover and turning the real paper pages.

Now, this may have seemed ironic. Many people read my books in paperback format. Real covers. Real paper pages. The tactile reading experience. And yet, here I was advocating getting rid of our books to downsize into a living room unit filled with our records. Another person might have pointed out the irony and prolonged the discussion. But Loren didn't. She was a bigger person than that.

"What's our alternative?" I asked. "Is there even an alternative?" I wondered out loud. I saw none, and she offered none.

We were moving to Denver. If it was wine, we could have investigated an offsite wine storage unit like you might see as you enter a Capital Grille restaurant. Lord knows what they cost!

If it was clothing, we could store the winter items when it was summer and then switch out as the winter snow arrived.

But it was neither. We would either have books or records. Despite that, we had no consensus.

Until I pulled five records from the shelves: Boz Scaggs's *Slow Dancer* and Hall and Oates's *Abandoned Luncheonette*. College favorites. Records we listened to several times a week sitting in Loren's Merion Hall dorm room after we first met. Those would surely tug on Loren's nostalgia heartstrings. Chuck Mangione's *Feels So Good* and Michael Franks's *The Art of Tea* were law and veterinary school favorites we listened to many times each week after studying. Our entry into jazz. And the deal sealer was Lou Rawls's *When You Hear Lou, You've Heard it All*, which we listened to every Sunday morning as we read the *Kansas City Star*.

I asked, "Are we ready to send Boz and the Luncheonette and Chuck and Michael and Lou to Goodwill?"

"No." Unstated was the conviction that we couldn't. They were us and we were them.

She could've made the case to stream "Slow Dancer" and "She's Gone" and "Feels So Good" and "Popsicle Toes" and "Lady Love" or keep small, narrow CD versions, but she didn't go there. That would be heresy. There was no heresy permitted at the kitchen table.

Books went back into U-Haul boxes and off to Goodwill the next day.

No tears shed. We moved to Denver shortly thereafter.

Today, we still have some books. But not many. Some I've written. Famous authors have autographed a few others. And a small number Loren rescued from the U-Haul boxes that night, and they made it to Denver without further discussion or objection.

We still have the vinyl records. All of them.

Which brings me to the title of this chapter. I've read that vinyl is back and vinyl albums may've even sold more copies last year than CDs and other forms of music.

How can that be? Simple. Vinyl's not "back." It never left. Not us. Not our 121 ½ inches of it.

Our NAD turntable seems happy. Our Revel speakers seem honored to pump out the warm sound of vinyl whenever we ask them to. Our Peachtree amp gives us good, clean sound no matter the format. Sitting atop the amp is a small Cambridge preamp, so we can hear the records as they play on our turntable. A technical explanation better left for another time, but the preamp is thrilled it has a regular job.

Sometimes, the warm sound of the record includes a hideous pop. Sometimes, the needle skips over a scratch.

What do we learn from that? Not that digital is better. We learn vinyl is imperfect. But that's okay. So are we. Maybe that's why we never switched to CDs.

The alleged perfection of digitized music on CDs just never seemed to fit with who we are. Maybe it doesn't fit with who many people are. Maybe that's why vinyl is back.

Maybe the world has concluded that analog is good. Maybe the world has realized analog is imperfect. Maybe the world now believes imperfection is in. If so, maybe that's a good start to a better world.

Or maybe it's just a warmer sound late at night with a glass of wine and a love close by.

26

Guitars & Me

JUST WIRE AND wood, some bone, some metal frets, mother of pearl, and some lacquer. Yet it sounds so rich, it feels so special; it acts so lovingly; it fills my days.

The acoustic guitar.

My particular love is a Martin D28, mine ushered into this world in late 1990. So it's about thirty-four years old. A child among wood instruments, but it's grown up nicely. Before me, it had an owner in Maine and then one in Wichita. The Wichita owner loved the guitar but needed cash. I gave him the cash and promised to take good care of his kid . . . and I have.

The cash was important to him, but the promise maybe even more.

Every day that I take it out of its case and play, I'm reminded how lucky I am to have it in my life.

∽

Christian Frederick Martin established C.F. Martin & Company in 1833, and it's still a family-run business today. Its headquarters and primary factory are in Nazareth, Pennsylvania.

First training as a cabinetmaker in Germany, C.F. moved to Vienna and apprenticed with a well-known guitar maker and began to make the instruments. When cabinetmaker guilds challenged his right to make guitars, he moved to New York City in 1833 and began his guitar-making legacy.

He centered his guitar innovations on using X-bracing, an element of design that supported metal strings. He then used a "dreadnought" body style, larger and deeper than previous acoustic guitars, which also supported fourteen clear frets, not just twelve. The sound from the larger body was smoother, richer, and more powerful.

The dreadnought innovation led to the development of the Martin D28 in 1931. At first, guitar players didn't favor its size. But it became wildly popular with folk singers and rockers in the 1950s and 1960s, so much so that during the 1950s, a buyer could wait two years before taking delivery from Martin.

The dreadnaught design shares its name with a type of large battleship equipped with six or more guns, each of twelve-inch calibers or more. I've always thought of the guitar as an instrument of peace. How odd to have a battleship share its name? But the name was intentional. The recently retired chief executive officer of Martin, Chris Martin IV, recalled: "The Dreadnought was considered the first all-big-gun ship. That's why I love to call our dreadnought 'a big gun.'"

∽

I started with a New Haven, Connecticut, pawn shop guitar. It came with no case. I don't remember the brand. Not big. Not fancy. Nothing like a battleship. Not a rich sound. But perfect for me.

When I wasn't sitting on the edge of my bed playing, it leaned against a wall in the bedroom I shared with my younger brother. One afternoon, he was acting rambunctious and ran into the guitar, knocking it to the ground. The side of the guitar that rested under my right arm when I played split lengthwise.

What Makes Me . . . Me

I locked my brother out and cried alone in the bedroom. I figured my parents would never spring for a new guitar. So when I finished feeling sorry for myself, I tried to glue the split back together as best as I could. After my crude repair, I could play it, but it buzzed, and the glued wood was rough, cutting my forearm on more than one occasion. But even on life support, the guitar was still there for me and still my best friend.

For my birthday, my dad surprised me by taking me to a music store and buying me a replacement. I had that for years until I bought a LoPrinzi guitar while in college, a handmade acoustic crafted by two New Jersey brothers, Augustino and Thomas LoPrinzi, who formed their company to ride the 1970s wave of acoustic guitars fueled by the 1960s surge first in folk music and then acoustic rock.

I had the LoPrinzi until the D28 came into my life.

⁓

As I've written about before, when the piano left my life and the guitar entered it, my mom didn't favor my new passion. With only six strings, how could it possibly compete for my attention with a piano? Much later in life, I learned Bruce Springsteen didn't have a family that loved guitars either. He said, "When I was growing up, there were two things that were unpopular in my house. One was me, and the other was my guitar."

Who could have guessed that The Boss and I had something as personal as the guitar and our family experience in common? Maybe there's hope for me yet.

⁓

I've played the guitar for over fifty years. I'm not world-class, I'm not on tour, I don't play in a band, but it's my thing. I have a couple of Fender electric guitars and a Guild as well, all of which I love, but my true first love is the Martin.

Here's what I've learned: the first time you pick up a guitar and play it, your fingertips hurt. It's as if the guitar has rejected you as its friend and makes you come back again and again to show your sincerity and earn its trust and love. Eventually, if you don't give up, your fingertips develop callouses, allowing you to play for longer and longer periods. One day, you notice that the guitar has accepted you, even offered you its love, and in its own way, lets you know you're a keeper. How? That rich tone it gives you back when you play it. That's when you know you'll be hooked for life.

Joan Jett said, "My guitar is not a thing. It is an extension of myself. It is who I am." So true. So mine lives in our bedroom, and I suppose it sleeps with us every night.

It's my friend and my confidante. My therapist and colleague. My collaborator and my creator. It's pop. It's life.

Its back rests against my body near my chest when I play. Right next to my heart. Where else should it be?

27

Tremé—The City with a Storm in Its Future and a Twinkle in Its Eye

"Welcome to the city that care forgot." *Tremé,* the HBO series.

This was New Orleans after Katrina. And yet, it's a city that always seems to survive. That survival comes with a twinkle in its eye, like one of its own, Fats Domino. We see it on our many visits there. It's in the music, the food, and most of all, the people.

Tremé captured that twinkle.

The series ran for four seasons, beginning in 2015, ten years after Katrina. The show picks up in New Orleans not long after Katrina and follows an ensemble of relatable characters as they try to put their lives back together after the storm.

Can one series capture a city as diverse, suffering, and complicated as New Orleans and do it justice?

Yes.

A (Way-Too-Short) History:

The series takes its name from the New Orleans neighborhood of the same name, also called the Faubourg Tremé or Tremé / Lafitte. Scholars describe Tremé as the oldest Black neighborhood in the United States where free Blacks could settle in the 1800s.

Tremé was the home to Congo Square, the place where Black slaves gathered on Sundays to play music and dance and where many scholars accept that it's the birthplace of American jazz and later exported throughout the country and then the world.

Much of New Orleans' rich musical heritage—Mardi Gras parades, marching brass bands, Mardi Gras Indian Big Chief chants, second lines, and jazz funeral processions—ran through Tremé before making its way to the rest of the world.

If you visit, you'll see streets of original shotgun homes and Congo Square, and you can imagine the suffering of Blacks that continued long after the 1865 emancipation through to today.

One cannot overstate the neighborhood's importance in American culture and history, and *Tremé* the series does an admirable job of bringing it all to the forefront.

The Series:

The series is about the single most endearing quality of the city and its residents: humans rising above impossible conditions to survive and thrive even in the face of the unimaginable horrors of everyday life and disaster.

It's the ability to survive and thrive that is the city's twinkle in its eye.

The series shows us this survival through a healthy and authentic dose of music, New Orleans style, food, and tradition. *Tremé* handles the horrors as well: the aftermath of Katrina; relatives and friends washed away by the storm; prejudice, violence, and corruption.

It doesn't spare us from the killings, looting, suicide, property destruction, FEMA's failures (the intro to Season Two contains a graffiti image: "Someone is getting rich. **F**ix **E**verything **M**y **A**ss"), and graft and corruption as fraudsters, business people, and politicians intercept and divert federal funds earmarked for recovery efforts.

It shows us this dark side by mixing real news clips of the flood waters, violence, loss, and political duplicity and draws us into the frustrations of a great city left to recover without sufficient support from the rest of the country.

The show mixes this dark side with stories of people surviving and thriving and it's in this regard that *Tremé* shines as it shares with us the city's music, food as only New Orleans can do it, love, Mardi Gras, and tradition.

It uses real-life New Orleans musicians in the cast who recorded all the music live for the show. The music and the musicians are a treat. Some musicians who appear are world-famous, including Dr. John (Mac Rebennack), Fats Domino, Allen Toussaint, and Marcia Ball.

Others may only be known to the aficionados and the locals, including John Boutté (who sings the wonderful theme song), Kermit Ruffins and the Barbecue Swingers, Trombone Shorty, The Rebirth Brass Band, Tremé Brass Band, and Coco Robicheaux. At all times, *Tremé* honors many of the architects of the New Orleans sound, including The Neville Brothers, Dave Bartholomew, Irma Thomas, Jean Knight, Kid Ory, and Professor Longhair.

What is it about New Orleans music that makes it so special and that *Tremé* captures so accurately? Apart from its rightful place as the birthplace of American jazz, it's also one of the seminal cities that gave us rhythm and blues, led by Fats Domino and his swing/blues-style piano bass lines beginning in the late 1940s.

New Orleans music is happy and hopeful and rich and emotional. It gives us a feeling of optimism, even when everything around us screams that nothing good is coming. Fats embodied New Orleans. Paul McCartney remembered him: "As one of my favorite rock 'n' roll singers, I will remember him fondly and always think of him with that twinkle in his eye."

You can see Fats's twinkle in every New Orleans musician, from those who play on corners on Royal and Bourbon Streets to those who play in Jackson Square to the local, no-name bar and music venue scene to the more famous venues like Tipitina's and Preservation Jazz Hall. You can see that twinkle in every chef and restauranteur serving up their own special take on New Orleans cuisine.

Even in the face of Katrina, you can see that twinkle everywhere you look. A twinkle like that is hard to capture in film, but *Tremé* manages to.

That was the point of bringing *Tremé* to the screen. Everyday people surviving as best they can, so often through their music.

It's my thesis that you just can't listen to New Orleans music without at least tapping your feet and singing along, if not jumping up and swaying and dancing. We tapped and sang and swayed along to all four seasons of *Tremé* as we binged it. I sat and googled every musician I didn't know who appeared on the show to learn about them.

The last episode of season four left us longing for more.

Maybe it's the chorus of John Boutté *Tremé* theme song that best captures the twinkle and the dichotomy of waking up to a storm-ravaged city every day while still making room for the traditions of everything that makes New Orleans so special:

Down in the Tremé. Just me and my baby. We're all going crazy. Buckjumping and having fun.

We love New Orleans and try to visit every year around the holiday time. I don't know how we missed seeing this series when HBO released it, but it's highly recommended for anyone who loves music, history, food, human survival, and New Orleans.

You can learn a lot about a person by understanding and listening to the music they listen to. If you want to know some more about me, find some New Orleans music to take in. I bet you'll tap your feet, and then you'll know right away where I'm coming from.

28

Spiderman & Iron Man

You can learn a lot about a person from the superheroes they loved as a kid (and maybe still love as an adult).

Early on, I was a Superman fan, watching the black and white show on WOR Channel 9 in New York City, starring George Reeves as the man of steel. I never missed an episode and could recite the voice-over introduction word for word (I still can today).

But while I'll always like Superman, he wasn't my superhero love. My two loves were (and are) Spider-Man (yes, it's spelled with a dash) and Iron Man (yes, it's spelled with no dash), both Marvel Comics creations from the minds of Stan Lee and his Marvel cohorts.

Spider-Man, a.k.a. Peter Parker, came to life when a radioactive spider bit him. Right after the bite, Peter, a Queens, New York, geeky teenage loner, could climb up the sides of the Manhattan skyscrapers and use the spider webs he created to swing between the buildings.

In the original storyline, he moonlighted as a photographer for the *Daily Bugle* newspaper, working for his bullying managing editor, J. Jonah Jameson. Upon the death of his uncle, Peter decided to use his superpowers for good, not self-gain or evil. He always tried to do the right thing, but the authorities struggled with whether he was a good guy or a bad guy, or maybe in our conflicted world, a good bad guy or a bad good guy.

The Spider-Man character has always been a fascinating presentation of a different kind of superhero: one who struggles with love, loss, and his own imperfections. Me too. Prior to Spider-Man, many of the superheroes were near perfect. Take Superman: he could fly; he had x-ray vision; he was stronger than any ordinary man; he came to Earth in a capsule from a faraway planet. He was comfortable in his own skin, and everyone (except the arch criminals) in Metropolis loved him.

Superman's only weakness was Kryptonite, which sapped his superpowers if he got too close to a chunk.

Apart from Kryptonite, Superman had few flaws. Not Spidey. The Marvel writers riddled the character with flaws. Just like me, which I suppose is why I like him so much.

He grew up in Queens like I did. He was a wallflower in high school like I was. He was a geek and totally self-conscious. Yep, me too. All he has ever tried to do is to find his way in life. Aren't we all in the midst of that?

Spidey seemed to have an inferiority complex. I'm simpatico with that trait. He was accident-prone. Me too. Peter photographed to make money. Check (although Peter shot for the crime beat, and I've been mostly about sports). What few powers I have, I try to use for good, not self-gain or evil (but sometimes I'm sure I'm a bad good guy or even a good bad guy, and therefore, like Spider-Man, I confuse the authorities).

But sadly, that's where the similarities end. Dream as I might, I never mastered the ability to climb up the side of buildings or swing between them on spider webs. Long as I might, no radioactive spider has ever bitten me.

So, unlike Peter / Spider-Man, I'm relegated to non-super, non-hero status. At many points in my life, I've found that a bummer.

What Makes Me . . . Me

And then there's Iron Man. Stan Lee once described his thinking behind Iron Man as making an unlikable character likable and may have based the character on Howard Hughes. Tony Stark, a.k.a. Iron Man, inherited his family's business after a car crash killed his parents. The company, under Tony's guidance, developed high-tech military equipment. After shrapnel damaged his heart, he developed a suit of armor that sustained and protected him and a device to keep the shrapnel away from his heart. He lived with an electromagnetic insert where his heart once functioned.

Along the way, he lost his company, became an alcoholic and homeless, gained back control of his company, and became a technological wizard, expanding beyond military equipment. And of course, he was a genius billionaire playboy.

Wow. Crazy plot line.

The Stark character always interested me. So human. So much life experience. So many ups and downs. So much gained and lost. So unlikable, even though he did so much good.

Always reminding the reader that what you have today might be gone tomorrow.

Unlike Peter Parker, however, there are few similarities between Tony Stark and me. My heart is fine; I'm a tech idiot; I like to tell myself I'm mostly likable (although when I practiced law, I suppose some of my law partners would debate that point from time to time). I'm not an alcoholic and I've not experienced homelessness. And—sigh—no need to even address the genius-billionaire-playboy mantra.

So what can you learn about me from Spider-Man and Iron Man, apart from the similarities and differences I've highlighted?

The most important thing is that I like to dream and enter the universe of my imagination as often as possible. Comics gave me the chance to retreat there and they still do. And that's a good thing. A very good thing.

29

Bionics—Steve Austin, Jaime Sommers (. . . & Me?)

My body now contains so many parts I didn't have when I came into this world.

As science fact catches up to science fiction, I'm thinking it's just a matter of time before I cross over to bionic status. Then I'll be more like some of my television heroes of old. I'd welcome that.

Most recently, I had a partial knee replacement. It's my fourth artificial part: left knee, left hip, cataract surgeries to implant new lenses in both eyes. I now have serial numbers for each of my manmade parts that I keep in our safe. My parts aren't bionic, but I like to joke that they are.

Bionics, of course, is a real thing, defined by Merriam-Webster as "having normal biological capability or performance enhanced by or as if by electronic or electromechanical devices." A cyborg is a bionic human.

Cyborgs are a favorite in Hollywood and some of the famous ones include Darth Vader (*Star Wars*), RoboCop, Seven of Nine

(*Star Trek: Voyager*), and the Terminator (the one played by Arnold Schwarzenegger).

And my all-time favorites: Steve Austin and Jaime Sommers, *The Six Million Dollar Man* and *The Bionic Woman*.

To prepare for my knee rehabilitation and to fill the time each day I was wrapped in ice machine pads, I bought the complete Blu-ray series of *The Six Million Dollar Man* and its spin-off show, *The Bionic Woman*.

Watching fifty-year-old Hollywood productions showcasing artificial limbs and body parts seemed the right thing to do after the installation of my new knee parts.

Y'know.... They just don't make cyborgs like Steven Austin and Jaime Sommers anymore.

Who were the original bionic man and woman?

The Six Million Dollar Man series ran from 1973 to 1978, the heyday of my television-watching years. Col. Steve Austin, played by Lee Majors, was an astronaut injured in a NASA test flight accident. The introduction to each episode of the *SMDM* went like this:

> Steve Austin, astronaut. A man barely alive. Gentlemen, we can rebuild him. We have the technology. We have the capability to make the world's first bionic man. Steve Austin will be that man. Better than he was before. Better... stronger... faster.

Doctors rebuilt Austin (at a cost of $6 million in 1973 dollars) and gave him limbs that could run sixty miles per hour and an eye that could zoom 20:1 with an infrared feature I never understood. His bionics left him with superhuman strength in one arm. The power of a bulldozer. Capable of inordinate feats.

After the doctors reconstructed him, Austin left NASA and became a spy, working for the Office of Scientific Intelligence (OSI) headed by Oscar Goldman, played by Richard Anderson.

I don't have as many new parts as Col. Austin received, and

I'm sure I'm not faster than I used to be. But my parts do make me better and stronger. Science is amazing.

Atomic energy powered Austin's bionic parts. My new parts are powered just by Mark. I'm not radioactive. I never understood why Austin wasn't glowing in the dark, but that's the beauty of science fiction: make it plausible without filling in all the blanks.

The Bionic Woman ran from 1976 to 1978. It starred Lindsay Wagner as the top-ten professional tennis player Jaime Sommers. Austin and Sommers went to school together in Ojai, California, and when they reunited, they fell in love and got engaged. They went skydiving and she was severely injured when her parachute failed.

Full disclosure. Some of my friends had posters of Farrah Fawcett Majors or Raquel Welch in their bedroom, but Lindsay Wagner was the object of my youthful crush.

At Austin's insistence, OSI saved Sommers's life with bionics, and after the surgery, like Austin, she ran faster and was stronger. Unlike Austin, she could also hear better because she received a bionic ear.

In a bizarre twist, her body rejected her bionics, and OSI led both Austin and the audience to believe she died of a cerebral clot.

The next season, OSI let us know she didn't die. Rather, OSI had placed her into suspended animation until the doctors could remove the clot. When they did, she had a degraded memory. Another surgery restored her memory except for one recollection: her love for Austin.

Crazy? I know. But it was the number one show in Britain and the only science fiction show to achieve that status in the twentieth century.

The shows were perfect, mindless "good guys win" television series that were broadcast during a time when America wanted their spies to win. A kind of made-for-TV James Bond hour on a budget with a little science fiction tossed in. Nothing too deep. Nothing too controversial. Escapism at its best. Sometimes silly storylines.

But Wagner's character was impactful. As she noted in a *People Magazine* interview: "It was the beginning of changing the image of women in the media." In a later interview with the *Desert Sun*, she said,

> There wasn't any prime-time show that starred a woman in the dramatic area. There were a couple people who were forerunners in the comedy area, but not a serious role and certainly not in a man's role, so "The Bionic Woman" kind of broke that glass ceiling and then all of a sudden there was a flood.

While we didn't appreciate the glass ceiling Lindsay Wagner was breaking during our first few years in college, my roommates and I gathered around our ten-inch black-and-white television to watch the shows. It was good, empty-headed fun to take our minds off of Political Science, Chemistry 107, Shakespeare, Economics, and Physics.

Each week, we left behind our studies for a short while to watch Col. Austin and Jaime Sommers use their bionic parts to save us from the bad guys.

Sure, it was campy, but America and Britain loved it. We loved it.

As I watched, I loved the chance to wonder what it would be like to have artificial body parts like Jaime and Steve. Little did I know.

SMDM and *BW* were right time/right place shows. They wouldn't get past the network executives today. Things have changed. Then and now are so different.

In 1973, some were still committed to fighting the spread of communism in Vietnam, while others were looking for a way out soon to be implemented.

Today, the Vietnam War is a notation in the history books with one lasting effect: it still guides politicians to come up with ways to engage in conflicts around the world without getting too directly involved.

In 1973, the Cold War was alive and well. It ended in 1991 when the Soviet Union dissolved (although it seems like the Soviets and the Cold War are back today and very much at it).

SMDM showed up on television only four years after Neil Armstrong stepped out of the lunar module, *Eagle*, to walk on the moon on July 20, 1969, and we celebrated that the space program had nothing but upside. We seemed to have a Buzz Lightyear attitude: *To infinity and beyond.* There was nothing we couldn't do.

Today, we still send astronauts into space, but NASA and the space program no longer seem to hold the same allure as they did in the '60s and '70s. We focus on what we can't do and can't afford to do. Except maybe for Elon Musk, Jeff Bezos, and Sir Richard Branson.

And, of course, in 1973, we had Richard Nixon at the helm. Crazy politics. Today . . . wait . . . maybe politics isn't a good example of how different 1973 and today are.

In 1973, we still seemed to be a hopeful society. I wonder about that today. I wonder about it a lot.

The *SMDM* and *BW* shows from fifty years ago are now dated. The 1970s' special effects are . . . well . . . not very special.

Austin and Sommers pumped their arms as they ran in slow motion to depict their superhuman speed, while in the background, we heard a strange staccato, echoing, percussive sound, I guess to let the viewer know atomic-powered bionics had taken over.

The 1970s' slow motion was nothing like watching today's *The Flash* movie and knowing that when Barry Allen runs across the silver screen, it's exactly what supersonic speed looks like.

But the big delta between then and now is this: what was science fiction fifty years ago is science fact today. Technology like the HAL 9000 computer in *2001: A Space Odyssey*, an artificial intelligence computer, is now accessible to any of us by navigating to ChatGPT online.

Star Trek's 1970s wireless communicators are our mobile devices today.

Artificial body parts are now a regular part of our lives, extending our quality of life for decades. Look at me. Look at artificial hands and limbs.

They don't make characters like Steve Austin and Jaime Sommers anymore. Instead, they put a bit of each of them into older folks like me and give me back some of my way of life. Just like OSI did for Austin and Sommers in the 1970s.

Maybe I have them to thank for my serial numbers and new body parts.

If so, thanks so much! I'll take that. I'd also take a little of that nuclear atomic energy to power me if they're offering it up anytime soon. I'm ready to cross over to cyborg.

30
Masters of the Air

In 1945, the world, except for Germany and Japan, seemed to like us American folks. Today, much of the world doesn't—except now Germany and Japan do. War has a way of turning everything inside out and upside down. Enemies become friends. Friends become enemies. The needs of the moment dictate who we stand next to and from whom we stand apart.

What might seem simple to the average Joe—good versus evil—is a complicated slice of world politics and diplomacy.

Hollywood can't design a limited television series to deal with the global politics and diplomacy issues that are brought on by, or the cause of, war. The best the viewer can hope for is a series providing a fair insight into one facet of war.

Masters of the Air, a recent series on Apple TV+, captures the inside outs and upside downs of World War II and focuses on the tribulations of the Air Force pilots flying bombing missions in the European Theatre. The miniseries is based on the 2007 book of the same name penned by Donald L. Miller.

Originally the brainchild of Tom Hanks's and Steven Speilberg's production companies and developed by HBO, the show had been in the works since 2012, when in 2019, HBO backed away from the series and Apple TV+ entered the scene and cut a deal with the production companies to move forward with it.

The show is an entourage drama with many stars. My personal favorites were Austin Butler as Major Gale "Buck" Cleven, Callum Turner as Major John "Bucky" Eglan, and Isabel May as "Margorie "Marge" Spencer. Butler was a Disney Channel teenage heartthrob, and of late, has developed a lengthy resume, including appearing on Broadway. Turner is a British-born actor whose career has seen him take on more and more significant roles. May's face and voice are well known to many since she starred as Elsa Dutton, the lead character in the Paramount+ show *1883* and narrated *1923*.

The show follows the 100th Bomb Group flying Boeing B-17 Fortress airplanes from eastern England. The military tasked the group with flying highly dangerous daytime missions to destroy strategic targets in German-occupied Europe. The Fortress planes were four-engine heavy bomber aircraft developed in the 1930s. These planes dropped more bombs in World War II than any other aircraft. The B-17 was a high-flying, long-range aircraft and was the third most-produced bomber in history.

For nine episodes, Apple TV+ takes you on a ride inside these World War II fighter planes as they fly into enemy territory to drop bombs on strategic targets. I rarely watch war shows. Certainly not bombing shows. But I watched this series and came away amazed.

Without giving away any spoilers, the series does an admiral job of taking you inside the B-17s as the crews fly missions and into the minds and personalities of the flyboys who manned them. You sit up front with the pilot and copilot as they navigate through German antiaircraft fire. Flack is everywhere. The tension is palpable, as is the pilots' calm in the face of impending death. You sit below as the bombardier prepares to drop bombs, and the navigator, without the aid of technology, determines the course and signals when the bombardier should announce "bombs away." Everything is so manual and analog, a time long since passed; it seems so real as the story's battles unfold.

The show addresses several World War II themes: the horrors of concentration camps in Germany as the war reached its end, prisoner of war camps where some flyboys ended up after capture, the infamous late-night wartime marches of prisoners for twenty miles as the German captors abandoned their prisoner camps and moved to outrun the allies who closed in, and the plight of the Tuskegee Airmen, the African American military pilots.

The cinematography is outstanding. You feel like you're flying in the cockpit, plotting the navigation course, shooting down enemy aircraft with onboard guns, dropping bombs, evading and taking enemy fire, dealing with engines burning from enemy hits, parachuting out of a disabled plane, mourning the loss of fellow crew members, and trying to escape capture by the enemy.

As you "sit" in the aircraft, you're leaning left and right to help the pilots avoid antiaircraft fire from the German ground forces. You and the crew just barely escape getting blown up in midair. And, in some scenes, you and the crew don't escape the fire as your plane blows up in midair.

It's just extraordinary. Heart-racing.

The series transports you back to the mid-1940s as Germany begins to lose the war. The series captures the period so accurately, including Benny Goodman-style swing jazz at the officers' clubs and period hairstyles. The show conveys the intensity of war and pulls no punches about the dangers the flyboys encountered in flying the B-17 missions.

The cast is outstanding. Actors playing World War II flyboys did their homework and nailed the danger and raw emotion and what it must have been like to be a member of the Bomb Group.

The script is outstanding. I focus on lines as if I were reading a book and try to appreciate the author's observations and creations. I'm moved by lines that I wish I had written. The story of any writer: "Gee. I wish I wrote that line." Those are the ones that stay with me.

I'm not sure if the following lines are the screenwriters' or Donald Miller's from the book, but here are some memorable favorites:

- "If you gaze into the abyss, the abyss gazes right back at you."
- "Whoever fights monsters should take care not to become one." (My favorite line from the series.)
- "Today is tomorrow."
- "Here stupid means dead."
- "You're a clever fella, Alex. But don't let smart be the enemy of happy."
- "Some believe there is a difference between war and senseless murder. [The Germans] don't."
- "You know, all this killing we do, day in, day out, does something to a guy. Makes him different, not in a good way."
- "The judge of life will judge you for life."
- "He says if God exists, He has forgotten him. Not even the earth that covers our bones will remember us." (Spoken by a Polish refugee.)

These kinds of thought-provoking lines inspire me to come up with ways to describe things and make them interesting for the reader. In that way, maybe they can make me a better writer.

I highly recommend the series. Whether you're a history buff, a World War II buff, a fan of war movies, a writer looking for inspiration, or even none of the above, *Masters of the Air* will not disappoint.

It made me wish Apple TV+ would drop all the episodes in one evening so I could stay up much too late and binge-watch the entire series, the true test for me of a magnificent series.

Observations, Reflections, & Opinions

31

We Know What You Had for Breakfast

WHEN MY WIFE and I applied for TSA's Global Entry, we scheduled a TSA interview at the Seattle-Tacoma International Airport. It should have been routine. It was disquieting.

TSA conducted the interviews at an upper level of the airport we had never been on. Up there, it seemed hotter and more humid. The light flickered, emanating from hanging tube fluorescent fixtures installed in days gone by.

If it had been in black and white, it would have looked like a Season One set from the original *Mission Impossible* television series.

We made our way to the only open door. The room was dimly lit, almost dark, except for the light coming from a lamp on one desk. We took a seat and waited for the TSA agent to call our names.

While we waited, he interviewed someone ahead of us in the queue. The interviewee was loud. The agent was mostly silent—listening. I'll call them Ms. Jones and Mr. Agent, not to protect them; I just don't know their names.

Oddly, Ms. Jones did most of the talking without the agent

posing questions. She regaled Mr. Agent about the number of decades she was a heavy cannabis user. She told him she still smoked and that she had even smoked that morning before coming to her interview.

I was a practicing attorney then and based on my experience, the interviewee was violating a cardinal rule of depositions—volunteer nothing. Answer only the questions asked. It was my credo as well—the attorney's version of what Harper Lee once said when declining an interview after writing *To Kill A Mockingbird:* "Better to be silent than be a fool."

Here was Ms. Jones prattling on (and on) about her life and her relationship to pot, all to a federal agent carrying a sidearm who swore to uphold the law of the land.

This land. The one where cannabis is still illegal on the federal level and, as of the time of the interview, was still a classified drug on par with heroin.

Now, do I accept it should be so classified and a federal crime to possess pot? I do not. I wondered if Ms. Jones needed an attorney to protect her from herself.

We never heard Mr. Agent say a word. The Ms. Jones interview ended. She left. From his desk, he said loudly, "Loren and Mark Shaiken." He mispronounced the last name as *Shie-ken*, but I didn't protest. I just wanted him to grant us Global Entry status, and to get that, Mr. Agent could pronounce our last name any way he wanted.

We came around a gate into the desk area and sat in two chairs set up to face the agent.

Mr. Agent sat facing us behind an enormous Dell Computer monitor. I wasn't sure why he needed that size monitor, but there it was.

Indeed, it was so large we couldn't see his face. Not if we craned our necks around the side of the monitor and certainly not over the top of it. Behind the top of the Dell, all we could see was a patch of thinning, sandy brown hair sticking up.

What Makes Me... Me

We sat and said nothing. After decades of marriage, Loren well knew my "volunteer nothing and make no fool of yourself" credo. So—silence was the order of the day.

I had seen attorneys do this Mr. Agent sort of thing in depositions. Shuffle papers, pretend to read notes, and say nothing while the witness sweated it out across the table.

Did it work? I have no statistics, but in my experience—no. All it did was piss off the witness's attorney sitting there, hoping the testimony would be short, to the point, and then over.

So we waited.

After an eternity (less than a minute), the head behind the monitor asked: "So you're a lawyer, eh?"

Loren is a veterinarian, so I deduced the agent had directed the question to me.

"Yes."

Not "yes, sir." Not "yes" followed by a rambling explanation of law school, my practice, my firm, my partners, and my clients. Just "yes." I answered the question he had asked and waited for the next one.

More silence. Then, "Looks to me like you're a bankruptcy lawyer. That right?"

Well, now that was interesting. The forms we filled out didn't ask me what kind of law I practiced. Indeed, sitting there, I couldn't even remember if the Global Entry form asked me what I did for a living.

"Yes," I answered. Credo at work again.

"So you help people get out of paying their debts?"

"I don't follow you." Credo number two: the witness should always ask the examiner to clarify a vague question.

"What part don't you follow?"

Ooh. A little testy. "I don't understand the question."

"I'm just asking if you help people get out of their debts. It's one of those yes or no deals."

Another credo of mine: don't let the examiner dictate how the witness must answer the question. Here, yes or no. So, rejecting the guidance to answer just yes or no, I said, "I practice bankruptcy law, as you seem to know. I help businesses reorganize, and if that means they end up paying less than they owe under the U.S. Bankruptcy Code, then I help them follow our federal law."

"I see. Hmm."

I could hear him rubbing the stubble on his chin. It sounded like sandpaper.

"So tell me," I said, now abandoning my credo (attorneys make terrible witnesses), "How would you happen to know I'm a bankruptcy attorney?"

He leaned to his right (our left), looked around the monitor, the desk lamp lighting only one side of his face, locked eyes with me, and said, "Friend, we know what you had for breakfast today."

Interesting. Friend? Not a friend of mine. I went back to my credo; he went back to his centered position behind the Dell and resumed the state of silence that seemed to pervade the interview.

Maybe he was mulling the next steps. Maybe not. But after a few more silent moments, he said, "That's all. You can leave." No "thank you." No "we'll be in touch."

Since we weren't under arrest and were there voluntarily, of course we could leave. Anytime we wanted.

We stood, Loren said, "Thank you," violating my credo, and we turned and left.

We said nothing until we got back on the Link to head north to meet our son for lunch. On the Link, Loren asked, "What was that all about?"

"Beats me. He didn't ask you a single question."

"Maybe he was an animal lover and wasn't worried about the veterinary profession."

"And he was worried about the law business? It was an issue?"

"Maybe so. Must've had a bad bankruptcy experience, or he doesn't like people not paying their debts. I bet we don't get Global Entry because you help businesses who can't pay their debts."

"Maybe so. Maybe we should've told him we smoked pot and were high." We didn't and we weren't.

"Maybe so. Maybe that would've helped."

Weeks later, TSA approved us for Global Entry by email. I would sure love to know who Mr. Agent was. Would love to know if Ms. Jones also got approved.

Recently, coming back from Norway, we entered the United States at O'Hare in Chicago. Global Entry there is quick and painless. Facial recognition equipment checks you out, and we flew through the process. Painless. Except every time I re-enter the U.S. through Global Entry, I remember Mr. Agent and wonder if we'll pass him someday, manning the Global Entry or customs lines.

I hope not. I bet he has an excellent memory.

There are times I wish housing in Vancouver wasn't so darn expensive.

32

Shaking the Ketchup Bottle—Bringing Back the Anticipation

I thought of adding this to the Pop Culture section. After all, is there any condiment more iconic, more American, more pop, than ketchup? But, it landed here. My suggestion? Read it with some French fries and ketchup (or catsup if you choose).

Do you remember the Heinz Ketchup commercials where a teenager tips a bottle and some thick ketchup slowly makes its way out and onto a hamburger and fries? The background music is Carly Simon singing her mega-hit song "Anticipation."

The years 1977–78. Back when ketchup was really thick, bottles were really glass, and the wait for the red sauce to engulf the food was really satisfying.

I was such a ketchup person back then. Still am. After sixty-eight years on Planet Earth, I count myself something of a ketchup aficionado. And a Heinz loyalist. A lifetime user of the Pittsburgh company's sauce.

Heinz packaged the sauce in glass bottles dating back to 1889 and even patented its own octagonal bottle in 1890.

Maybe you've noticed (and maybe you're as bothered as I am) that these days, most of the ketchup bottles are plastic squeeze containers. Heinz introduced these squeeze demons to restaurants in 2002. At around the same time, the glass bottles disappeared from the supermarket shelves.

I am *not* a fan of the plastic squeeze containers.

Globs of ketchup squirt out intermittently, sometimes spraying everywhere except on the burger and the fries. Ketchup collects at the squeeze apparatus, dries out, and looks gross.

And maybe it's just me, but I can never get the last of the ketchup from the bottom of the plastic squeeze bottle to the top so I can squirt out the last bit I paid for at King Soopers.

Folks may consider my dislike of the squeeze bottle one of the many signs of old age. Rants. More and more of them as hair thins. This one is in the category of "set in my ways." And in the subcategory of "why fix what ain't broken."

But I like progress. I like my laptop, and Apple TV, and my mobile phone and text messages, and Medium.com, and EVs, and heat pumps, and Lightroom and Photoshop, and mirrorless cameras (Nikon of course), and Sonos, and a host of other advancements.

I'm generally forward-looking. But not this time. For me, this squeeze thing is deadly serious, and it's not just the complaint of an old geezer.

Let me be clear: I've had it with the squeeze bottle industry. And recently, I got so mad as hell that I wouldn't take it anymore.

I needed to take action.

I bought a glass bottle and started the experiment of making my own ketchup. A full-day project. Several saucepans on the stove going at the same time, simmering different versions of recipes and ingredients identified after many Google searches.

The decision to make and bottle my own sauce didn't come without consequences. There was thick red sauce everywhere.

Stovetop. Countertops. Some bubbled onto the kitchen floor. Some sprayed onto my shirt and jeans. "Ketchup is great on hamburgers, but if some gets on your shirt, that does not make your shirt also a hamburger." – *Bill Engvall*.

Bill had a good point. But this was no time to stop the project. I was so close to my goal, so I pushed through the mess. I could circle back to cleaning up later.

I cooled the different batches, tasted them, tested them to make sure they had the right thickness, and settled in on one batch that came pretty close to what old Henry J. Heinz must've had in mind in the 1880s at the dawn of his glass ketchup bottles.

My batch was also probably not too far off from what Carly sang about in the late 1970s commercials. I'm sure she must've been a ketchup fanatic as well. Why else would she lend her song "Anticipation" to promote Heinz ketchup? Money, you say? Maybe, but she had principles. So it might be both: primarily a love of ketchup and secondarily the money.

Back to *my* ketchup. Having perfected my recipe and cooled my sauce, the moment of truth had arrived. I poured my mixture through a sieve and then through a funnel into my tall glass container. Mine wasn't hexagon-shaped like the Heinz bottles of old, but then again, I wanted to respect the Heinz patent, of course.

Once I filled the container, I poured the rest of my sauce into a Mason jar and froze it for later use.

I made a grilled cheese sandwich (Kraft American cheese), turned on Carly singing "Anticipation" on the stereo (Sonos), and, keeping the sandwich open-faced, turned the glass bottle upside down and waited for the ketchup to slowly make its way out of the bottle and unto the cheese.

Ahhh. Perfection. Just like the commercial. Glass. OMG. Words escaped me.

If I could right this wrong in one day in my small kitchen, why couldn't Heinz? Just this one small thing to make an old guy like me smile.

But I'm sure Heinz won't. I wonder if the problem here is that in 2013, Berkshire Hathaway and a Brazilian investment firm bought Heinz for twenty-three billion dollars. That's a whole lot of ketchup they'll have to sell to recoup the enormous investment. Maybe plastic squeeze increases the return on investment. I don't know.

I may have to bring this to the attention of Warren Buffett, the Oracle of Omaha. Warren, are you reading this? Please bring back the glass hexagon bottles!

33

I Can't Keep Up

1961: "How DID you watch baseball when you were a kid, Grandpa?"

"We didn't watch, boychik. We listened." ("Boychik," a term of endearment in Jewish households, was the nickname given to me by Grandpa Jerry.)

"You mean on the radio?"

"Right. Come here and let me show you."

Grandpa led me to another room in his house. There was a large wooden piece of furniture, a box with a dial on it. It was the size of a television cabinet. He flipped a switch, and it came to life. He turned the dial, generating a hissing noise until the game came on.

I had heard the radio, of course, but we had a small television in our house, and I *watched* baseball. I didn't *listen* to it. We had a radio in the house that sat on the top of the refrigerator. My mom and dad listened to it a lot. Background music. Frank Sinatra and Johnny Mathis offerings. By the early 1960s, radios had shrunk as transistors were on the horizon.

"That was the Golden Age of Radio, boychik."

"Golden Age?"

"Right. We sat by this radio. We listened to the president of the

United States tell us we had nothing to fear but fear itself. Do you know what that means?"

"Sure, Grandpa." I didn't exactly know, but I wanted him to think I did.

"We listened to music. New American music we had never heard before played by musicians who were new to us. Swing jazz. Count Basie broadcasting live on Friday night. Duke Ellington broadcasting live on Saturday night. We also listened to the Grand Ole Opry. Country. Roy Acuff. The Fruit Jar Drinkers. All playing right there in our living room on this radio."

I nodded.

"We listened to radio shows."

"Radio shows, Grandpa?"

"The Battling Bickersons. Soap operas. Flash Gordon flying around. The Shadow."

"But you never saw the actors?"

"No. We closed our eyes, listened, and used our imagination to envision what the scenes and characters would look like if we could see them."

"Now we can see them, right Grandpa?"

"Right."

"Does that mean we'll lose radio, Grandpa?"

"I hope not, but time marches on. Things change. I don't like it, but I don't have much of a say in it. Hell, we've got men flying around outer space now."

"Without radio, will I lose my imagination, Grandpa?"

"You? I doubt it, *bubula*. You'll keep up with all the new stuff and still imagine. Me? I'm pretty sure I can't keep up with all these changes."

༄

2024 (sixty-three years later): I talked to our son recently about the modern era of new things I was having difficulty understanding. Change was now happening at a pace I couldn't keep up with. I wanted to tell him about the radio conversation I had with Grandpa sixty-three years ago. I didn't. I was worried he would tell me he'd never seen a radio in a large cabinet . . . or black and white Humphrey Bogart movies.

"Kiddo, what's all this crypto stuff?" ("Kiddo" was the nickname we had given to our son.)

"I'll send you some links, Dad, to articles you can read."

"Can't you explain it to me?"

"Not really. Just read the articles. You'll get the idea."

"Kiddo, do you know how fast things are changing?"

"I guess not. What do you mean?"

"I'm a baby boomer, right?"

"Sure."

"Have you ever considered the last hundred years of change—of all the new ages?"

"I guess not."

"When I was born, television had just started. That was the big change. That and a car in every driveway. No internet. No electronics. No streaming. No social media."

He listened politely. He'd heard me talk about "the olden days," as he called them.

"I've now lived in many ages. The continuation of the age of the humans. The age of space exploration. The nuclear age. The internet age. The technology age. The age of the superpowers. The age of mass shootings. The age of social media. The age of climate change. The age of the pandemic. The financial crisis age. The fake news age. The Internet of Things age. The Dot-Com Bubble age. The age of the influencers. And if you're into astrology, the age of Aquarius (just like the song in *Hair*)."

"What's that got to do with crypto?"

"I guess nothing and everything."

"Okay. Now I have no idea what you're talking about."

"The ages are each a change. They seem to come at a quicker and quicker pace. One after the other. Learn about one age and the next thing you know, you're in the next one. Dillydally in understanding the new age you're in and it'll have passed before you ever figure it out."

"So don't dillydally, I guess."

"I'm trying to stay up on everything. I'll read the crypto stuff. I'm sure I still won't understand it. I guess there comes a point where I don't need to understand all the ages and all the changes."

"Maybe not," he said, sounding more and more like he had other things he'd rather be doing.

"Maybe we can watch some black and white movies sometime."

"Sure, Dad."

"Or maybe we could listen to 1940s radio recordings of Count Basie? You know, mix the old and the new. I'll read about crypto and you'll learn a little about your grandpa and great-grandpa."

"Sure. Whatever you say. Hey, I gotta run."

"Okay. What's on your agenda today?"

"I'm writing some code to help speed up financial transactions for my team at work."

"See. There it is."

"There's what?"

"Change. Code. Financial transactions. The age of computerized financial transactions. Sounds new and exciting. I hope you enjoy it."

"I like it but it's work, Dad. Gotta go."

"Love you."

"Love you too. Hey Dad?"

"Yes?"

"Read the crypto articles. We can talk about them afterward."

"Thanks, kiddo."

❧

I found the crypto articles. I reflected on how I would read them. With my laptop computer, I clicked on a link my son sent me in a text message that connected me to the world and maybe even outer space. I streamed. I searched. I learned. I played. I listened. I watched. Jumping from site to site, event to event. Article to article. It was remarkable.

But, when I read the articles, I confirmed what I already suspected. Crypto had served its function for me. Its function wasn't to give me new and faster ways to conduct financial transactions.

It showed me I can't keep up with all the changes.

34

Let the Darkness Out

LET THE LIGHT in.

Maybe we can't. Not until we let the darkness out. Until we do, we live in dark times.

In a lament about the ill effects that social media has had on society, I heard someone say that we once were a society of civilized conversations. But now, social media provides a forum for those who don't want to talk or listen. Just yell louder. At everyone. At no one. At each other. We want to win all arguments, at times, by any means necessary.

I hear the lament. I understand it. I'm not a huge fan of social media (and its owners), but I can't blame social media. We've never been a society of civilized social discourse. We've always been a society practiced in the art of crushing differing opinions and then feeling good about it.

Our history has so many examples. Here are some that have resonated with me:

- The 1863 New York City draft protests that devolved into a race riot between Irish immigrants and Blacks to silence the protestors.
- The 1913 suffrage movement that beget assaults on the suffragettes by those opposing a woman's right to vote.
- Citizens deputized by the local government who, in 1921, destroyed Tulsa's "Black Wall Street," where Black business thrived.
- Joseph McCarthy, who silenced political beliefs, ended careers, brought out some of society's darkest fears about religious groups and destroyed lives in his quest to root out alleged communist elements from society through his House Un-American Activities Committee in the 1950s.
- White supremacists, who violently tried to impede the 1963 Selma to Montgomery march.
- The Chicago political machine that violently put down the protests at the 1968 Chicago Democratic National Convention.

Our founding fathers granted us freedom of speech in our Constitution's First Amendment. We all know that. But they didn't direct us to listen. And we don't. They didn't advise us to respect differing views. And we don't. Not before social media. Not on social media. We have freedom of speech and freedom to publicly ignore and disrespect anyone else who speaks.

Without listening and respecting, there's too much darkness and light struggles to shine in.

While it seems hopeless, I still hope that there is still hope.

What's right? I hear you. Hear me. I respect you. Respect me. Pretend as if the Constitution mandates it. If we can just try it, we'll go a long way to letting the darkness out. Once we do that, there should be room for that ever-elusive light to shine in.

35

Wins & Losses

I was in the wins and losses business for many years. The practice of law. We've all grown up in a wins-and-losses world.

In the law, we ask, "Did I win that case? Did I save the client some money? Did I make some money for the client? Did I win that motion? Did the negotiation turn out well for the client?"

Answer yes to any of the questions and it was a win. Answer no and it was a loss.

It's not just the law. Each day, we're inundated with reports of wins and losses. The standings in the sports section of the newspaper each morning tell us if our favorite home team is in first place or last. These days, we can also see an almost endless volume of metrics that analyze and explain the wins and losses.

The newsfeeds tell us in real time which politician is doing well and which is struggling to get votes.

These days, virtually any item for purchase has a star rating. We buy the widget with a 4.7-star rating, and we reject the one with a 3.1 rating. The food articles in the news apps tell us which wine won a gold or silver medal and how many points it garnered in a tasting.

If winning doesn't matter, the newsfeeds didn't get the memo.

The newsfeeds know that winning and backing a winner makes us feel good. So they pump us full of the stories about winning and losing that we lust for. We can't get enough.

We also have our own personal ledgers that we keep. We note how many likes we get on Facebook. Likes make us feel good. We note how many impressions we get on LinkedIn. Impressions make us feel we're not alone, even when we are.

If you write books, you read the reviews. The positive reviews are wins. The negative reviews are losses.

We introduce our kids to winning and losing early on. In rec league sports, on television, on their report cards, and when a college accepts or rejects them. At every turn, they compete, and in many households, they're encouraged to be a winner and implored not to be a loser.

Did Russell "Red" Sanders get it right when he famously told his football team (and us) that "Winning isn't everything. It's the only thing"? Or, years later, did Lionel Messi get it right when he disagreed and observed, "There are more important things in life than winning or losing a game"?

Of course, Lionel failed to list those other, more important things, and maybe it's easier to downplay winning if you're Lionel Messi and rarely lose.

For what seems like an eternity, we've debated these points in the court of public opinion with no clear winner (or loser).

Winning and losing are not standalone notions. They're integral to each other. They have a symbiotic relationship. They feed off of each other. One can't exist without the other. The recent loser dreams of winning someday. If we didn't play to win, we couldn't also have a loss recorded for posterity. The recent winner knows that "without losing, winning isn't so great." – Alyssa Milano.

Winners have parades to celebrate and share the win with their fans. They give victory speeches to throngs of cheering fans spread out as far as the eye can see.

Losers shower, dress, pack up, and go home to wait for their chance to try to win next year.

Fans storm the field when their team wins a nail-biter. Fans leave early when their team is losing. We honor our winners and dismiss our losers.

Winners land on the front page. Losers may not even get a page.

From an early age, we're taught that it's more fun to win, and people don't treat the losers the same way they treat the winners. We learn it's just more satisfying to do something better and have the world reward you for it. I once heard Jim Palmer say, "Losing is no disgrace if you've given your best." Great advice, but I bet Jim knew precisely how many games he won during his Hall of Fame Major League Baseball career. It was a lot. Two hundred sixty-eight of them. I'm just wondering if he had enough experience with losing to have the expertise to support his advice. I wonder if giving your best is enough, or is it enough only if you come out on top?

Over my law career, my clients, my law firm, the judges before whom I appeared, opposing counsel, and my colleagues at the firm kept track of my wins and losses. It made the practice of law a competition.

Who had more billable hours? Who had more clients? Who won more trials? Whether I *wanted* to keep track of wins and losses, I did so because I had no choice. Everyone else seemed to keep track, so I needed to, if for no other reason than to make sure their tally was accurate.

I kept track, but I never liked the win-loss ledger.

֍

Now I'm in my next season, *My Life 2.0*. It's a delightful feeling.

Nothing makes me keep track of wins and losses, and maybe I shouldn't, but, damn it, I'm still doing it. I know how many views and reads I've gotten on Medium. Thanks to KDP and ACX, I know how many books I sold today. Thanks to Goodreads, I know how many readers liked my books.

Why? Why am I still putting myself through the ledger thing? Habit? Maybe. Healthy? Unclear; perhaps not. Human nature? Apparently so. Too late to change? Undoubtedly. Should I change? Perhaps . . . but certainly not until I see how many folks on Medium read my pieces and I digest my daily KDP book sales report in real time.

Just saying.

I feel like I give it my best pretty often. And when I do, and things don't work out, and no one reads my Medium posts or no one buys my books, I don't feel disgraced. Just ignored . . . and not much like a winner. Not a good feeling even in *My Life 2.0*.

So, maybe I need a moratorium. Perhaps tomorrow, I'll take a day off from keeping my win-loss ledger. I won't look at my stats for the day. Yes, that's it. I'll give that a try . . . if I can stand it.

36

Lessons from the Northeast

I WAS A Northeasterner once. I first left in 1978, returned in 1988, and left again in 1991. I haven't lived there since. Even after I left for good, the coast continued to talk to me. Maybe to teach or remind me of some imperatives. I tended not to listen, but now that I'm older, I listen every once in a while. Here are four things it's said to me of late.

Number 1: As I've reported before, for my first six years on Planet Earth, we lived in a not-so-great 1950s neighborhood in Queens—four of us in a small, one-bedroom Elmhurst apartment.

When I visited the Lower East Side's Tenement Museum a couple of years ago, I realized small is relative. Our Elmhurst apartment was spacious compared to my family's Lower East Side, Brooklyn, and Bronx experiences when they first arrived from Russia.

When I listen, the coast says to me, "Be happy with what you've got, dude. It could always be less and things could always be worse."

My response: so true.

Number 2: Also, as I've reported before, we moved to New Hyde Park on Long Island when I was six. There, I had friends, baseball (the Mets), and my black Schwinn. After five years, we left with no warning on December 10, 1965. "That Day," as I refer to it.

I might have missed the memo from the parents to advise of the impending event, but I kinda think there was no memo.

So, no goodbyes to friends. The parents just showed up at school one morning, walked me out of class, and off we went to a new life in southern Connecticut.

Except for one friend with whom I reconnected decades later, I never saw a single NHP friend again. I used to be angry about That Day. Even though they orchestrated That Day, my parents were also angry about it and spent the rest of their adult lives trying to return to New York City.

Strange.

Eventually, they moved back. Eventually, I moved on. From time to time, the Northeast says to me, *"Enjoy what you've got while you've got it because you've no right to it or anything."*

My response: Hey. I hear ya.

Number 3: New Yorkers are gritty. I'm not now. I'm not sure I ever was. When I visit New York, I find the chaos of getting from point A to B so bewildering.

Frank Sinatra (and others) sang that if you can make it there, you can make it anywhere. Frank's attempt at a lesson. But, in that line, I always heard this lesson instead: "If you can't make it there, you can't make it anywhere."

If that's what the Northeast is trying to teach me, my response is this. On this one, I must respectfully disagree. There are many other anywheres, and in a few of them, I've made it.

Number 4: When Timothy McVeigh and Terry Nichols bombed the Oklahoma City federal building on April 19, 1995, I learned Oklahoma Citians were the toughest people in America.

Then came 9/11. New Yorkers were already tough, but on that day, they joined the OK Citians as the toughest people in America (later to be joined by New Orleans residents when Katrina made landfall in August 2005).

Back then, I had a big case in bankruptcy court in Manhattan. Each month, I'd travel to the city the night before my court appearance and stay in the Millennium Hilton across from what would become Ground Zero.

On one trip, days before 9/11, I had dinner with Father Mychal Judge, the New York Fire Department chaplain, at his favorite restaurant in Little Italy. He was gracious enough to spend hours with me talking (and then driving me around Manhattan) as he counseled me about family matters. I'm not at all religious (and I'm not Catholic), but as he talked, his personal prayer bubbled to the surface:

Lord, take me where You want me to go;
Let me meet who You want me to meet;
Tell me what You want me to say;
And keep me out of Your way.

He died at the Trade Center days later on 9/11, racing into one of the burning towers and into harm's way to save people.

I suppose he would have said that at dinner, he delivered his words to me because his God encouraged him to. I'm not sure about that. But those words repeat in my head from time to time as if the Northeast needs to make sure I don't forget them. And in them, the Northeast's (and Father Judge's) lesson seems to be: "Honor, respect, cherish and love each other and our differences. Recognize what connects us."

My response: Good words. You were a wise man, Father Judge. I didn't know you well, but I know I miss you and the prospect of more meals in Little Italy and drives around Manhattan.

37

Those Low-Down, Nasty, Good-for-Nothing COVID-19 Blues

YEAH, YEAH. I read the news. I know the pandemic is over. But there's more to the story. Like so many, I heard the COVID Blues playing in my head when the pandemic first struck. They've been playing there every day since, pandemic or no pandemic. For the longest time, I didn't learn the song. But now I know it by heart, and it goes something like this.

On March 3, 2020, a friend and I went to a Denver Nuggets basketball game. A week later, we were all in lockdown. Two months later, my friend was dead. Of COVID. Not contracted at the Nuggets game, but dead nonetheless. Weeks later, another close friend ended up in a coma on a ventilator for weeks. I don't know how he did it, but he lived.

At the time, we lived in downtown Denver in a forty-two-story high-rise. Overnight, our beloved downtown went from a vibrant, busy, exciting place to live to deserted ribbons of concrete and asphalt. No conventioneers. No restaurant crowd, no art and music lovers hitting the streets after an opening or performance.

What Makes Me . . . Me

None of the two hundred thousand workers who came to work downtown every day. No one in the RTD trains. Everything that made downtown Denver special was on hold or gone. The streets were apocalyptic. The only people on the street below were the homeless, sad and gut-wrenching to see as always, but now with no one around from whom to pan for money. All alone on empty streets in an empty downtown, patrolled by Denver's police in SUVs, with automatic weapons drawn to deter looters.

When I looked out over my downtown from my cave high above, I was sad, and like Puff the Magic Dragon, my scales fell like rain.

At the Governor's request, beginning a few weeks into lockdown and every night at 7 p.m., downtowners opened their windows or went out on their balconies and joined the Governor in howling like wolves. A collective pack of thousands of people, strangers to each other, howling, the sound echoing through the empty downtown canyons as it bounced off the high-rises.

Somehow, for the longest time, my spouse and I managed to avoid the vile virus, but I couldn't avoid the song. It played on even as we employed our strategies. We eschewed all notions of vacationing and eating out at restaurants. We saw no relatives or friends in person. I had dem blues.

Finally, after five vaccines and the arrival of Paxlovid, we felt sort of, kind of, maybe just a little, safe enough to head out on our first vacation. By then, those COVID Blues were playing only faintly in my head, and I hoped a trip along the Pacific Coast Highway would drown out the song—from Denver to Santa Barbara, to Paso Robles, to Carmel-by-the-Sea, to San Francisco, then Portland, and finally to Seattle to see our son and a friend, and then home. We mostly wore masks. We mostly ate outside. We mostly avoided crowds.

What could go wrong?

The night before our scheduled flight back to Denver, we arrived at our son's house, and I told him I was having a minor allergy attack. "You better test, Dad, just to be safe." Uh-oh. Hmm. Okay.

So I did, and I was COVID-positive. Two lines on a made-in-China test. I tested again. Two lines again.

And of course, those two lines changed everything. We left our son, donned masks, and headed for an airport hotel, hearts racing. Separate rooms. My Denver doc could call in a Paxlovid prescription to Seattle, which I started that Monday. But before Paxlovid took hold, my temperature spiked to just over one hundred three degrees.

With the high fever, I heard them COVID Blues playing again. Nothing faint about the music this time, and this time, I could see the whole band—the singer, the harp player, the drummer, the bass man, the keyboardist, and the guitarist—all dressed in black. Keening away to a driving beat, singing them COVID Blues. As the music played, I remembered that I had another book to write, and then, in conversation with myself, I realized I couldn't even recall the name of the next book or my star attorney who had appeared in the prior books.

I heard the singer sing, "Oh, sing them blues." I saw the lead guitarist close his eyes, lean his head back, and bend his strings to make the guitar moan those COVID Blues.

I talked to myself and wondered where I contracted the virus. I had no response. Instead, there was that song and the singer: "Oh baby, sing them blues."

I needed to sleep, so I laid down and the singer serenaded me, "Sing 'em. Sing them blues."

COVID relented and then I got the Paxlovid rebound. But what the hey. I lived. A cause for celebration. Then, more than a year after the virus, COVID's gift remained: high blood pressure, intense itching on my arms and legs, and the song at the top of the charts playing in my head. That song. Every day, I could still hear a guy blowing the harp, dressed in black, and the lead singer belting out them COVID Blues.

I guess it's a tune that gets in your head and then doesn't leave, whether or not there's still a pandemic. The gift that keeps on giving.

38

Laughing Instead of Crying & Other Things My Nanny Said

My grandmother, Edith Shaiken (Nanny Edie to me), and Grandpa Jerry ran a candy store and a soda fountain. She had a good number of Shaikenisms that she liked to say. Here are three that have stuck with me.

We were at one family get-together or another. Our family get-togethers differed from the way television portrayed families in the late 1950s and early 1960s. At our gatherings, people yelled at each other, agreed on very little, and smoked like chimneys. The cigarette smoke was so thick that in our 8mm black-and-white home movies, you could barely see the party participants. Too much smoke.

At one of those gatherings, a woman asked Nanny, "Edith, how can you laugh?"

"What?"

"I said, how in hell can you laugh at a moment like that?"

Nanny nodded, raised her eyebrows, and asked, "What should I do? Cry?"

This was an interesting one. We were at a party. People were everywhere, almost shoulder to shoulder, seeming to have a good time even as they argued and yelled. No one had died. No one had gotten sick. There were no obvious moments at the party.

Maybe the woman was referring to some past moment? Carrying the weight of challenging Nanny the next time they met?

I never saw Nanny laugh when someone died, got sick, or suffered an injury. People complained. She nodded. Grandkids got hurt. She tended to them. People were hungry. She fed them. People died. She mourned. But she must have laughed at some point in the past, and one woman deemed it inappropriate.

Despite the vagaries of the rhetorical question, it's still fascinating to me. I'm mindful that, "it's harder to laugh than to cry." (Henry Thomas, the child actor in ET, said that). With that in mind, I've dug out the phrase and used it when things were going bad in life. The rhetorical question more profound and richer than the dismissive phrase "it is what it is" or the aggressive "shit happens." The "cry response" suggests a life of suffering where one could cry about everything because almost everything happening is bad. Instead, one laughs it off and moves on.

It's like a verbal shrug. The modern-day "I've seen worse" or "get over it."

My Nanny Edie was deep in her own way.

One time, my dad took me to the candy store Nanny Edie and Grandpa owned. Dad knew what I wanted: a vanilla milkshake while I sat on the cushioned, shiny silver pedestal chairs that went round and round. He made the best milkshakes. Breyers ice cream with the black specks of vanilla, milk, and more vanilla syrup than any kid should drink. All dropped in a stainless steel canister and then churned in a mixer like the Hamilton Beach retro mixer you can buy today on Amazon.

While the shake churned, he put out a soda fountain glass while my grandpa and Nanny went up and down an aisle, taking inventory. Grandpa bent down to see the lower shelf and came upon an item for sale he hadn't ordered. He stood up, looked at Nanny, and asked, "Who the hell ordered this, Edith?" She put her hands on her hips and didn't answer him. He shook his head and as he moved on, he said, "It'll never sell. Who would ever buy it?"

"Jerry, if you nail two pieces of wood together, some shmuck will buy it. Eventually."

Another Shaikenism, I guess. Perhaps she simply meant "hope springs eternal" or "have faith" or, more likely, "you don't know what the hell you're talking about."

Any of these would fit the moment.

One time, I was visiting Grandpa and Nanny in their Brooklyn house. We had moved to Long Island by then, and in our little town, there were outbreaks of antisemitic remarks made by several kids at the schoolyard to the handful of Jewish kids in attendance, like me.

I complained to Nanny about it and said it was the reason I wasn't getting picked to play on the softball team during recess.

She shook her head slowly. "Come over here and sit on my knee."

I did.

"Have you heard the story of the Jewish man who wanted to be a radio announcer?"

"No, Nanny."

"A Jewish man sees an ad in the *Daily News* for a job as a radio announcer and decides to apply. He goes in for an audition, and that night, tells his wife he's excited that he might get the job. A week later, he gets a letter in the mail, and it says the radio station hired someone else. The man is distraught, and that night, tells his wife this:

'I d-d-d-d-d-in-t-t-t-t g-g-g-g-et th-th-th-e j-j-j-j-j-ob b-b-b-b-b-cause I'm-m-m-m-m J-J-J-J-ew-ish-sh-sh.'

"You see, Mark. He didn't get the job because he had a bad stutter and that wouldn't work out too well as a radio show announcer."

"Not because he was Jewish, Nanny?"

"Maybe. But maybe he just needed to work harder to figure out a way to get what he wanted even though he was Jewish and even though he stuttered."

"So what should I do?"

"Run faster. Hit the ball farther."

"That's it?"

"Yep."

"Okay, Nanny. I'll try."

Funny how you can hear things as a young kid and they stay with you even when you become an old man.

She was a wise candy store lady indeed.

39

The Empty Stadium

I PHOTOGRAPH MAJOR League Soccer. Now that we live in Denver, it's the Colorado Rapids. Before that, in Kansas City, it was Sporting Kansas City.

It's an exciting game. Fans are loud and passionate with a European and south-of-the-border flair. They fill the stadium with synchronized cheers, chants, and songs to root the Burgundy Boys (the Rapids) or the Boys in Blue (Sporting) on to victory.

Some chants:

- *"I'm Blind. I'm Deaf. I wanna be a ref."* It's pretty self-explanatory what leads to this chant.

Or

- *"I"* - *"I believe"* - *"I believe"* - *" I believe that we will"* - *"I believe that we will win."* Repeated over and over just as the game starts in a call-and-response in Children's Mercy Park.

Or

- *"Over there, it's so quiet. Over here, it's a riot. We're walking along, singing our song, walking in a Rapids wonderland"* sung to the "Winter Wonderland" song.

Or

- *"We all bleed Rapids burgundy, Rapids burgundy, Rapids burgundy" (two times), "Ole Ole Ole Ole, Colorado, here we go" (two times)* sung to the Beatles' "Yellow Submarine" song.

Or one of my favorites:

- *"Today is Monday (Today is Monday). Monday is a drinking day (Monday is a drinking day). Does that make you happy? (You bet your ass it does!) Da da da da da"* chanted in a call-and-response and going through all seven days of the week as the game winds on.

And on and on. There are many songs and chants throughout MLS land. Crazy, fun, exciting, loud. Different from other sports. It's what makes soccer soccer.

But in 2020, as the pandemic unfolded, the MLS leaders first put the season on hold and then later decided the teams would play an abbreviated schedule in empty stadiums.

Here's what soccer without fans was like for me.

The Rapids afforded me a media pass. To enter Dick's Sporting Goods Park, I had to pass a rapid Covid test given at the stadium and wait fifteen minutes for the result. At all times, I had to wear a mask, whether inside or outside. When the vaccine arrived in 2021, I had to wear a mask and show my vaccine card to enter.

The team didn't permit the handful of credentialed photographers onto the field. Instead, the team moved us twenty feet back on a raised concrete area that, during normal times, was home to concession stands and tables for fans to eat and drink.

Twenty feet farther away from an already long field is a huge deal in sports photography, and my images from 2020 are not among my best. But it was vitally important to keep the players as safe as possible, and if that meant no close contact with outsiders like me, I was all for it.

I was lucky to have access to the games. I was happy for the chance to do something out in the world and happy to bring images to fans who couldn't attend in person.

Then, a COVID outbreak struck the team, and they had to suspend games while struggling to get and keep players healthy. It shaved weeks off the Rapids' already contracted season.

All of this happened just a few years ago, but as I sit here and write this account, it seems like it happened in another lifetime, just like everything else about the pandemic.

What's it like to be in an 18,000-person stadium with only the teams, the team staff, the coaches, the players, the referees, and a few photographers?

Eeerie. Unworldly. Bizarre. Fascinating. Quiet.

The virus-mandated empty stadium wounded, if not killed, home-field advantage during this phase of the pandemic. No fans, no noise, no chants, no songs. No advantage.

But the early pandemic also gave me a new access I had never had before.

During an empty stadium game, when the players weren't chirping on the field, I could hear a pin drop. But as the abbreviated season unfolded, I learned to hear many things that get lost in a loud, sold-out stadium. Like a symphony that had been playing all along but only revealed in the silence of an empty stadium. The music of that symphony was players yelling out a play, barking a defensive call for help on the wing, screaming at the referee, howling in agony at a missed shot, and celebrating a goal.

All in multiple languages. MLS is a very international league. I don't speak any language except English, but when the players speak in Spanish or French or any other language, in an empty stadium, it's not hard to understand what they say. So if a player swears in his native language, there isn't any question what he says and to whom.

Soccer is also a very physical game. With no background noise at all, my appreciation of the game grew. Revealed in the silent stadium was the commotion of heads banging each other, kicks to the shins, the ball ricocheting off the goalkeeper's gloves, and the gunshot-like boom of the ball coming off a kicking foot.

It was new and fascinating.

It's a kind of access I didn't get before the pandemic and I don't get today now that fans and my normal field access have both returned. The stadium is once again so loud that the symphony of the game revealed during COVID is hidden.

So it's back to "Colorado, here we go" and "I believe," and as much as I came to appreciate my access during the pandemic, the sport is not the same without the legions of the faithful, and I'm grateful that we're all back at it.

It's another lesson courtesy of COVID.

We can do what might have been unfathomable before the pandemic: live inside, alone in a small flat, waiting for the invention of a vaccine; pivoting to a work-at-home existence; communicating on Zoom; eschewing close contact with most humans; recording music with bandmates in faraway places; ordering home delivery of almost everything; wearing masks everywhere.

And, yes, not as much in the life-or-death category, but we continued to compete in sports like MLS while bringing games to fans on television, even games played in empty stadiums. I miss the pandemic symphony of the competition, but I missed the fans more. Professional athletes were meant to perform in front of live audiences, and photographers were meant to capture the action as it unfolds in front of 18,000 faithful.

40

Saving Us from Ourselves— Bomb Drills at Manor Oaks

JAPAN IS SUCH an amazing country. The people are so welcoming. Their warm feeling toward Westerners can be surprising, considering the United States dropped two atomic bombs there.

In 2017, my family and I traveled to Japan for the second time to explore the country from Tokyo south to Okinawa. We had purchased a rail pass on the Shinkansen, the Japanese bullet train, and rode first class. We crisscrossed the country, stopping in Kyoto, Nagano, to see the Japanese macaque (the Japanese snow monkeys), Kanazawa, Hakone, Fukuoka to see friends, and on to Okinawa for a cooking class and to see where the Army had stationed my dad in World War II. Then back to the mainland for Miyajima Island and . . . Hiroshima.

In Hiroshima, we made our way to Peace Memorial Park, the site of the detonation of the atomic bomb on August 6, 1945, the first of two dropped on Japan. In a stark reminder of the effects of the Los Alamos, New Mexico, Manhattan Project, the park is home to the A-Bomb Dome, the twisted metal and concrete skeletal remains of the former Hiroshima Prefectural Industrial Promotion Hall, one of the structural casualties of the "Rain of Ruin."

We can never put the unimaginable monster America awoke and let out back in the bottle.

The Peace Memorial Park not only reminds us of the victims of the bombings but also the horrors of the nuclear age. It advocates world peace. People go there to commune, remember, and pray.

Twenty-nine years and a month or so after the U.S. destroyed Hiroshima, my fourth-grade Manor Oaks Elementary School classmates and I huddled under our school desks, sitting cross-legged, heads bent, and hands on our heads. We were practicing what to do during a nuclear attack on New Hyde Park, New York.

Whoever in the school system had invented and mandated the drill had obviously never seen the A-Bomb Dome.

It was a solemn drill. Everyone in school practiced what to do at the same time in each classroom. Our teacher announced that we would begin the drill and asked everyone to take their positions under their desks. We did so dutifully. She walked around the classroom offering advice to tweak our form: "Johnny, pull your legs in closer to your body, please" and "Jill, remember to cover more of your head with your hands."

Johnny and Jill complied. Would those tweaks have made any difference in whether Johnny and Jill would survive a nuclear attack?

It was a strange time. Even stranger in retrospect. In 1964, our parents' generation was in its prime and had firsthand knowledge that America dropped the two bombs to end World War II. We were less than two years out from the October 1962 Cuban Missile Crisis. We huddled under our desks less than a year after someone assassinated President Kennedy. The Vietnam War was ramping up per our adoption of the domino theory to stop the spread of communism throughout Southeast Asia and then the world.

Daily, Walter Cronkite reported on the CBS Evening News that danger lurked around every world corner. Significant danger. This was the era of the Cold War, and Walter worried with us each evening in flickering black and white about our assured destruction, with the USSR and the U.S. pointing enough nuclear weapons at each other to annihilate everyone and destroy much of the world.

And there we sat on the floor, right after recess, cross-legged, under our old, heavily varnished grade school desks, taking direction from a well-meaning school teacher about how to protect ourselves if someone dropped an atom bomb on New Hyde Park.

Remarkably, our intelligent, highly educated parents not only approved the drills but spoke up at school board meetings to make sure the schools implemented them to protect the children.

None of the adults in the room apparently had looked at the A-Bomb Dome or any of the films of the Hiroshima destruction—the children whom the bomb melted alive; the vast, empty radioactive field created where the bomb detonated, replacing people and structures; the more than 100,000 Hiroshima lives lost, both from the immediate explosion and the long-term effects of nuclear radiation exposure.

Had they, I expect we would have called off the drills to protect ourselves from the aftermath of the Manhattan Project.

Perhaps the school board would have turned its attention from a foolhardy exercise of hiding under a rickety wooden desk to protect the children from a nuclear attack to a non-denominational prayer session each day, begging whatever Lord there might (or might not) be to save us from ourselves.

Perhaps a daily prayer session at such an early age would have been more impactful on a classroom full of fourth graders than shooing us under desks and then helping us with our form to better protect us from the A-Bomb.

We didn't and don't need protection from the A-Bomb. There was and is no such thing. We just needed, and still need, protection from ourselves. The drill was nothing more than an absurd exercise diverting us then (and now) from the hard work of protecting humankind from humankind.

We, not our implements of destruction, are the monster. Right?

41

The Legend of Honey Haverford

IN 1976, MY alma mater, Haverford College, a small Quaker school on mainline Philadelphia, was a single sex, men-only college. The school had a "cooperation" arrangement with Bryn Mawr College, a women-only Quaker college just down the road. Students at either school could take classes at the other, major at the other, and, subject to a room draw procedure, even live at the other.

Each year, Haverford received applications for admission from high school women that it turned away. The reason: no women allowed. "Let them apply to Bryn Mawr" was a sentiment you heard often. A debate began on campus and among the board of trustees. Should Haverford remain single-sex or should it go coed? Was it a legitimate reason to turn someone away based on their gender? Was that the Quaker way? Should the trustees bring to an end the tradition of institutional gender discrimination at a school where traditions reigned supreme?

That debate brought out some unfortunate viewpoints. Chauvinistic even by 1970s' standards. Ultimately, Haverford's board of trustees, with substantial student support, did the right thing and voted to make the school coed. Today, the student body is 54% women.

During the 1975-76 debate, I listened to some repulsive arguments about why women should never matriculate to Haverford. From 1975 to 1977, I wrote a sports editorial column for the *Bryn Mawr-Haverford News* called "Sports Queries." One column was a cynical article addressing the coed issue, transparently cloaked as a sports opinion piece. Of course, the piece had nothing to do with sports, but my editor ran with it anyway.

Today, the protagonist in my legal and financial thriller series is a Black woman making her way in a white man's law firm world. Still glass ceilings. Still repulsive views held by some, but hopefully, fewer and fewer, and with luck, the pace of equality for women and all other marginalized members of our society picks up.

I've thought about the glass ceilings, exclusions, and unfair treatment a lot since it came to the forefront at Haverford in 1975. And I've returned to my 1976 attempt to address the issue in my own way.

So here is that early attempt. I've done some 2024 editing to clean it up as bit, but some of the article is dated because I wrote it in 1976 as a teenager. As you read it, please keep that date and my age and my lack of sophistication in mind.

The Legend of Honey Haverford

Harry Stiles and Joe College arrived at the dining center and got in line. After a busy summer, they were back at college. They felt a different atmosphere. Something sinister, evil, and malicious lurked behind the closed Haverford doors.

After a nutritious meal courtesy of ARA, Joe and Harry headed for the bathroom (ARA food had that effect) and again got in line. Over lunch, they decided to meet later in the old gym to shoot some hoops and play some pickup games.

Harry arrived first at the gym. By and by, nine people trickled into the gym. They needed only one more to start a game. Suddenly, the ground shook, and the overhead track vibrated. Evil was close by. Then, in sauntered the cause of everyone's anxiety.

It was Haverford College's first coed! She was out of DeWitt Clinton High School in New York; big, mean, and owner of a shot that put fear into the varsity sharpshooter's heart. Recruited by the varsity coach, she stood six foot, eight inches tall and weighed in at over 200 pounds. This was the coach's magic ticket to an MAC title he'd been dreaming of for years.

After a brief discussion with his fellow male constituents, Harry relayed a message that she could play, but only until someone else arrived. Someone male.

It wasn't long until she awed everyone present with her basketball IQ and ability, possessing moves not yet invented.

Afterward, Harry approached her and discovered her name was Honey, Honey Haverford. Harry invited her to his room for a beer—Schmidt's, since it was local and Harry liked it better than Coors. Honey declined, surprised that Haverford athletes drank beer. Harry chuckled to himself, "Boy, did she have a lot to learn."

As the weeks went by, the legend of Honey Haverford spread far and wide. She was controversial, and her presence at the school brought many negative comments. She was, after all, not male, and her admission was a break in the sacred Haverford tradition. Traditions died hard at a school like Haverford.

The Saturday night before the opening varsity basketball game, Honey and her roommate, Jane Mueller, were in their Barclay dorm suite playing backgammon and listening to Boz Scaggs. Without warning, six Haverford student guerillas came in through the windows. Armed with water pistols, they were dangerous. They tied up Honey and Jane and declared, "A woman's place is in the home, not at our sacred school, competing with men."

After a scuffle, they threw Honey and Jane out of the window, and the coeds plummeted to their deaths.

Trust me, the preceding story is true according to some among our ranks. The names have remained the same because no one is innocent. In a male society, Haverford is a haven for male chauvinists who believe women perform best in bed. Women belong here, including those who play sports. The change in women's sports must come from the Harry Haverfords of today, the future armchair quarterbacks, who will see that women here will be a good thing. Maybe if we start today, by the time Haverford goes coed, the future Honeys of the world will play in their first game and some may make all-MAC. Maybe not.

In either case, the opportunity should be there, shouldn't it? If you don't think so, who are you to make that decision for the Honeys and Janes who want to come here for their education?

Aging—We All Seem to Be Doing It

42

I'm About to Be Old

I'VE BEEN OLDER for a long time. Next up—I get to be just plain old. But when does that officially happen? Soon. Quite soon. Here's how my "getting older" to "now I'm old" progression has gone.

When I turned the ripe old age of thirty, I took a day off from work to sit cross-legged on the floor of our Houston home and reflect on how my life was more than a third over. Lots of questions: Was I where I wanted to be in life? Had I done all that I had hoped to do by thirty? Were there things I wanted to do that now looked unachievable? What was the definition of old? More than halfway through life? More than two-thirds of the way? This was the age before the internet, so I could pose questions more easily than I could answer them.

I was young enough that I focused on getting older. Was I? "Perhaps," I concluded, but I was doing fine. Even if I had to admit I was getting older, at thirty, older was nothing more than a state of mind. Nothing to worry about for a very long time.

Getting old? Not even on the radar screen at thirty.

And . . . cross-legged? How lucky was I to sit cross-legged back then?

At forty, I had the beginnings of cataracts and was losing some of my precious sight. I moved to progressive bifocals that, over the next ten years, got more and more powerful as my doctor tried to combat the effects of advancing cataracts. I found it hard to drive at night. Oncoming headlights refracted and filled my field of vision, blocking out traffic and other road objects. Less driving mobility in a city of cars and little mass transit.

At forty, I wondered more seriously, "Am I getting old or just older?" I had fewer accomplishment questions to ask myself. I had reached the stage of "it is what it is" in my evaluation process. I had done what I had done, even if it wasn't everything I had hoped it would be. I told myself not to worry about things I'd never get to do.

Not a state of resignation or disinterest. A state of acceptance.

But I still played basketball, had little in the way of aches and pains, wasn't overweight, and was in shape. So, I concluded, "perhaps" I was getting older but not significantly. Nothing to worry about. And the eyes? Well, science would fix them and make my vision even better than before.

At fifty, my best friend and I met at our alma mater to play basketball. My plan was to play at least once in each of my decades. Playing on my fiftieth was an important milestone. We met, played, moved in slow motion, didn't get hurt, and even found some kinder young folks to play a few pickup games with the grandpa team—us.

That was just before my cataract surgery. Shooting a basketball with progressive eyeglass lenses was a trip (to use a 1960s slang word that has fallen out of our vernacular). Hard to shoot if you can't see the hoop.

That night over drinks, my friend and I, two freshly minted fifty-year-olds, contemplated the pace at which we were getting older.

For the first time, "old" had shown up on the radar screen, albeit a faraway, faint blip. Suddenly, the question of getting old was no longer an easy one to dismiss. It required thoughtful consideration . . . and some wine . . . to give it its proper due. It had graduated from a throwaway question answered with ease to a heavy (another 1960s relic) question with lots to consider. Soreness in the morning. Graying hair and less of it. Chub where once there was none.

Other system checks revealed: mind—still good; body—developing issues; eyes—to be fixed; reflexes—not what they once were, but acceptable; hair—don't get me started; wrinkles—yes.

Two unfamiliar words entered my vocabulary: minoxidil and retinol. Did they work? I was going to have to find out for myself.

And, for the first time, a serious consideration of the "am I old?" question was upon me. Older? Yup. Lots of changes in the present-day catalog. But I saw even more changes on the horizon. Was I ready to say I was old? Not yet. I was a fighter. I would take on Father Time and beat him back. Older didn't mean old at fifty.

Fade in the final Jeopardy music for the next ten years.

At sixty, many things had changed. Some positives. New lenses in my eyes. Cataracts gone; 20/20 vision returned. No glasses needed to drive, read, or watch television or movies. I didn't even own a pair. Mind—still functioning well enough to be an attorney and try cases.

Many negatives. Midriff—chubbier. Oh well. Hair—don't get me started. Wrinkles—check. Crabbiness? Check. In growing amounts, but old people—wait, I'm sorry—*older people* should be crabby. We all expect that from our elders. Sixty years on Planet Earth can do that to anyone.

And new, troubling signs: several surgeries on my left hand to enable me to keep playing the guitar. My left hip hurt. All the time, more and more. Thoughts of retirement and moving to my next season occupied my daily drive to and from work. Stiff every morning. Pain some mornings. I needed two cups of caffeine to jump-start the engine. Stress bothered me more. Too bad my job was all about stress.

For my sixtieth birthday, we flew to London for a week. The night before my birthday, we ate dinner near the Bank Street Station in silence. I looked up slowly and asked, "When the hell did this happen?" The next day, I turned sixty and cemented the understanding that I couldn't control my destiny. But even at sixty, while I could see the "old" lighthouse on the cliff beckoning to me, I wasn't there yet.

Then, I retired from the courtroom gig and moved on to writing. As I retired, I had occasion to consider more philosophically about nearing the "old" marker.

Older vs. old was now important to me, but once I reached my mid-sixties, I realized it was pure nuance, all part of the same process. Just different points on the matrix. I acknowledged to myself that I'd been playing a game of nuance for decades to help me deal with an ever-shortening timeline, and now, I could stop playing.

I had read articles about the latest craze—biological age vs. actual age. Measuring age based on how old cells and tissues are rather than a chronological age. Was I turning seventy soon, or did my cells say I was turning forty-five? I've contemplated going through some tests to see about my biological age, but how would I react if my biological age came back at eighty when my chronological age was sixty-five? My reactions: Betrayal. Confusion. Old. A sense science had denied me my chance to gracefully accept old age.

Biological age seems like a solution looking for a problem. Becoming old isn't a problem. It just is. A consequence of being born. It's as if someone in some university lab said late one night: "They don't want to be old. Let's just tell them that physically, they aren't old yet, even if they are. We'll call it biological age. Rife with uncertainties and plausible deniability in its calculation. Brilliant!!!!"

A recent *National Geographic* article surprised me by reporting that scientists quibble over what aging is and when it starts. It's not that hard, folks. It's being a year older each year. It starts the moment after we're born, doesn't it? What they should quibble about is whether there are things we can do to slow down aging, and if so, they should agree on what those things are. Until they do definitively, I'll just steer away from the biological measurement.

No tests for me. I'll stick with the dance partner that got me this far—good old (pun intended) chronology. My actual age. Sure, as that number gets higher and higher, I'll become more and more alarmed, and I'll do everything I can to squeeze every drop of juice out of this old lemon.

After almost seven complete decades, I've decided to set the date for next year (2025) as my official "I'm old" announcement (and party). When that happens, I'll be in later life and I'll be elderly. Officially a senior. Maybe even a geezer.

Again, all next year. Not now. I'm permitting myself to be categorized as "old"—*in a year-and-a-half*. Still, this is a significant moment. I've decided I can definitively say that I'm old, or will be soon.

Shouldn't I just wait until I'm old to declare that I am old? Isn't there a rule requiring this? If there is, that's fine and I apologize for breaking it. When you are about to be old, you don't have to follow all the rules.

You know what's convinced me that my "old" phase is about to arrive? For one, my chronological number is now alarmingly large, and my body reports to me I'm old when I wake up in the morning even as I'm quite grateful I'm still waking up in the morning. Two, it's become so obvious to me that all seventy-year-olds are old. Father Time will win. Little by little. We all lose. Like the old man in *The Old Man and the Sea*.

In addition, there are some worn-out parts in the chassis I've dealt with. Hip replacement surgery was followed a few years later by a partial knee replacement surgery. Yes. Two surgeries designed to give me back my mobility and, with it, my quality of life, convincing me I'm old.

The surgeons informed me the parts replaced, once functioning well, were no longer covered by the Mount Sinai Hospital maternity ward warranty plan given to me at birth. After a life of getting older, the parts had gotten old and had worn out. Now I have a new knee. New hip. New eyes. What's next? There are many other parts no longer under warranty that are probably hanging on by a hair.

Deep breath. Long sigh. Final Jeopardy music still playing.

Nothing wrong with being old, right? Almost all of us in the "about to be old" crowd like me say it all the time. You hear less of that, however, from the "already old" crowd. They know better. Soon, I will too.

So here's my sneak peek announcement: the "old" moniker is officially coming in 2025. At that point, I've decided (or at least hoped) that I can be old for a very long time. After all, I was "older" for a very long time, much longer than I was young. When my "old" arrives, I hope it doesn't mean I'm near the end, just *nearing* it.

I have lots left to do. For one, I have to play basketball, somehow, before I turn seventy. Once a decade, baby. I hope that's not a delusional aspiration of an old(er) person losing his ability to be rational. But for the record, I decided to play in each of my decades before I agreed to turn into an old man next year.

So, a pre-elderly, rational decision.

43

When All My Strands Are Gone

I USED TO wonder what would happen when my hair started thinning and falling out. Oh, I was well aware of what the signs would be: hair on my pillow in the morning. Hair caught in the shower drain filter. Hair in the sink. More hair in my hairbrush. Fallen hair now lying in places it had never lain before.

In the not-so-older days, most of my hair was where it was supposed to be. On my head sprouting out of follicles. A good mop. Reasonably thick. Reasonably long. Reasonably curly. Reasonably dark.

But like many other things as I've aged, the days of reason and reasonableness are in my rearview mirror.

Now, I have less on top and less each day that passes. A growing expanse of scalp revelation on which still sits some hair but in increasingly shorter supply.

I lose it from the crown. I lose it from the top. I lose it from the front. The round bald spot in the back grows. The front hairline recedes. Time marches on. Every single day.

I was an attorney, and there's a good reason male attorneys lose their hair. The practice of law is a hard, stressful job. Taking shit.

Giving shit. Having to give a shit all the time. All day. Every day. And too much of this kind of shit means much less hair on top.

Scientists may come up with perfectly reasonable scientific reasons for hair loss—heredity and the like. But I'm here to tell you it has more to do with shit than genes, at least if you practice or practiced law.

Law school didn't help either. It wasn't a job. It was worse. Work and stress beyond measure with no pay. It was tedious and expensive, and at many points over the three years, boring. It was just a necessary evil so I could practice law, but it set the tone for my later life hair loss.

Whether it's because of giving and taking shit in the practice of law or the ordeal of going to law school, no hair club, no weave, no strand-by-strand method, no minoxidil, no biotin, no miracle pill or application, no prayer, and no voodoo could stop the process.

Nothing could stave off the hair loss. Nothing.

Once I realized this, my choices were to join the "bald with dignity" association or to mask the problem. Masking? Defined as growing my remaining strands of hair longer and then twirling them around my head to cover as much scalp as possible or combing them over from around my ear upward to the top of my head.

That's a lot of work.

I didn't engage in masking. I decided I was a member of the Bald with Dignity club. Truth be told, with curly hair, I couldn't grow strands that allowed for a combover that would stay in one position.

So no creative combing for me.

But there are members of a creative combing club out there that work the strands each morning like twirling spaghetti. For these folks, there's no "bald with dignity" motto. There's no "skin is sexy" attitude. There's no acknowledgment that a receding hairline makes your head look bigger, and perhaps with a bigger head, you look smarter.

Instead, every morning, these men who are not in the Bald with

Dignity club make a futile executive decision to try to stave off the inevitable.

That's not me. That's not who I wanted to be. No. For me, thinning hair was just another opportunity to decline to let growing older (and becoming old) define me. And it's been a chance to reflect. Every morning, I look in the mirror and marvel at how much less hair there is up there. It's a sobering time of the day for me. I sigh.

I close my eyes and recall college days when I had a mop like Pete Maravich's hair. I remember watching Pete's commercials for Dry Control By Vitalis and the commercial's theme song: "He's using Dry Control by Vitalis. You can't see it, but you know it's there." A few moments of Pete playing basketball, spinning the ball on his finger and dribbling, and then at the end, he asks a beautiful woman who's resting her chin on his shoulder, "How am I doing?" She answers, "Stick to basketball."

Pete was my hero. Pete's gone. Sad. My hair is going. Also sad. Vitalis won't help.

So what can I do about this march toward a new not-so-great look? Nothing. The same thing I can do about getting older and all the attendant revelations and doctor's appointments that go along with that inevitability. I could lament some more but instead I must say goodbye. I have to run to see another doc.

44

Getting Old—The Golden Years Scam

SOME TIME AGO, they (the ubiquitous "they") told me that *when* I got old, I'd get better. They told me that my "old" period would be my golden years. I'd find those golden years over the rainbow, and they pointed to the horizon.

They lied. Fake news. Not better. Nothing golden. I looked at the horizon. No rainbow.

These days, old is not a matter of *when,* as if that's still a day off in the future. *When* is gone. It's been replaced by *now.* Or for me, almost now. Now is not better now. Now will not be better soon.

Better? To quote John McEnroe, "You cannot be serious."

Here's a list of some of the not-betters.

There's nothing better about having to adjust my diet. Spicy foods—on the way out. Fried foods—forget it. Coffee—I still love it, but it no longer loves me. For heaven's sake. What's next? Drinking Ensure three times a day?

There's nothing better about hearing my body talk back to me. No one can convince me that hearing my knee joint make audible cracking sounds when I wake in the morning is better. Better was when my knees knew their place and were silent while I drank my morning cup of Pu Erh tea.

There's nothing better about giving up jumping. Jumping is pure joy. Every kid from the earliest age can do it and they do it because it's so much fun. So affirming. Such freedom. No one can convince me it's better to be grounded to Mother Earth than to hang in the air waiting for gravity to take hold and bring me back down.

There's nothing better about not hearing things. Years of playing electric guitar have taken away some of my hearing. Not all of it, but some of it. This can't be better.

There's nothing better about getting confused. No one can convince me it's better to walk across our townhome into the living room with such purpose, and then, as soon as I get there, realize I can't remember why I needed to be in the living room. Then, as soon as I return to the kitchen, I suddenly remember why the living room was so important. No one can convince me it's better to make two trips when I used to need only one.

There's nothing better about forgetting things from the past. Someone once told me that to be a good attorney, you needed the memory of a goldfish. He meant I needed to forgive and forget. I've learned to forgive . . . sometimes. And now, forgetting is easy. No one can convince me that forgetting things that didn't involve forgiving is a good thing.

There's nothing better about needing to use my maps program to direct me where to turn for every single one of my driving trips. No one can convince me it's better to make sure I won't get lost when not all that long ago, I simply didn't get lost.

And there's nothing better about reading silly self-improvement quotes about getting old. The quotes are wrong. They're not inspiring quotes for us old folks. They're for the younger crowd who are worried about getting old. Here are some:

- Whoever said, "Aging isn't about slowing down; it's about ramping up" was wrong. A ramp-up is an increase. Nothing good increases when you're old. Things decrease. You slow down and you learn to live with moving slower.
- Whoever said, "Age is just a number, but attitude is everything" was wrong. They meant a good attitude. I've developed an attitude as I've gotten older, but it's not a good one. It's this: aging isn't for the faint of heart.
- Whoever said, "Aging is like a fine wine. It gets better with time. So raise a glass to your aging journey" was wrong. I'm able to drink much less as I age. Soon, I'll have to be a teetotaler, and whatever wine is left in my tank will pass through the fine wine stage and turn into expensive vinegar.
- Whoever said, "Aging isn't a curse; it's a gift" was wrong. A gift is something voluntarily transferred by one person to another without compensation. There's nothing voluntary about aging. I've gotten many gifts in my life for which I'm grateful. I know what a gift is. Aging is not one of them. A curse, on the other hand, is a cause of great harm or misfortune. Need I say more?
- Whoever said, "Aging is a reminder that life is full of infinite possibilities" was wrong. Infinite means extending indefinitely. Endless. Life's not endless. If I lived forever, then my possibilities would be infinite. But aging is a reminder that I won't live forever or even close to forever. It's a reminder of all the things I had hoped to do in life that I won't do because I'll run out of time. There's nothing infinite about running out of time.

∽

I don't enjoy characterizing the aging process as the seasons of a year. Spring, summer, fall and winter of life. That's made no sense to me.

What Makes Me . . . Me

It's not a good analogy. The winter isn't the end. It's what happens before the flowers bloom again.

Oh no! Now I'm sounding like a *Being There* Chauncey Gardiner character. I've also read much more about aging than I should. It doesn't make me feel better. I don't need feel-good platitudes and pithy sayings. I need honesty.

There. I've gotten it off of my chest and I don't know about you, but I feel better. I realize I've been on a rant in this piece but . . . I mean . . . Really?

Face it: aging is about getting old and then even older, and then dying. Here's how I look honestly at aging. It's learning to live in the moment. You have today's moment. You may not have tomorrow's. Just that simple. The future, once off in the distance, is now much closer and sometimes much scarier.

❧

I remember seeing Clark Terry, jazz great and flugelhorn player extraordinaire, perform live at Kansas City's Gem Theater for an organization called the Coda Jazz Fund. Coda raised money to help families of dying jazz greats pay for burial expenses. Clark was one of our jazz heroes. We had seen Clark perform live for many years.

He was in town to help Coda raise money.

He came out on stage, walking gingerly. We had seen him when he was younger. Then older. This time, he was just old.

He still had the infectious smile. He could still blow the horn like no other. But he couldn't stand well. So, he leaned precariously against a chair that was on stage for him to sit in. Refusing to sit for the first number, he played. Beautifully. The flugelhorn, with a tone mellower than a trumpet, is transformative in the hands of a jazz master.

After his first number, he looked at the chair, shook his head in disgust, turned, and addressed the audience: "I'm here to tell ya. The golden years suck." He got an enormous round of applause.

Then he sat for the next number.

Now there was an honest assessment of entering old age.

If there's a heaven, Clark is now there. Likely still playing, this time for the masses. Hey Clark, when it's my turn, if there's a heaven and they let me in, I'll hope to see you. We can discuss this whole golden years scam.

And don't even get me started on that damn rainbow. Don't point to the horizon. I've looked. It ain't there.

45

Doesn't Anyone Want to Be My Doc?

My draft Craigslist ad:

Wanted: Primary care physician. Board-certified in internal or family medicine preferred. I need one. I have none. I need you. As soon as possible. I'm old. I'm retired. I ache. I have prescriptions I need refilled. Dr. __ ? Please contact me immediately.

Act One – Scene One: We arrived in Denver in 2015, and after several physicians with whom I wasn't comfortable, I found a primary care physician whom I liked and trusted. She was in a four-doctor group practice, all PCPs.

In a telemed video call with her during the pandemic, she shared she was overwhelmed, and she calculated she would need thirty-seven hours each day to handle all her patients, calls, consults, and communications. I'm not a psychologist, but she seemed depressed.

According to the American Association of Family Practitioners, burnout is "a psychological syndrome in response to chronic interpersonal stressors on the job. The three key dimensions of this response are overwhelming exhaustion, feelings of cynicism and detachment from the job, and a sense of ineffectiveness and lack of accomplishment."

I was familiar with the definition, and I'd seen burnout in the law practice. She checked all the boxes. The practice had definitely burned her out.

Six months later, she left her doctor group and set up a concierge practice, charging her patients a fee of $3,000 per year for the privilege of having access to her. She also had decided not to take any insurance payments. All claims for insurance reimbursement were the responsibility of the patient.

The concierge fee was on top of the insurance premiums I pay. I learned Medicare wouldn't reimburse the fee, and many times, the medical services rendered.

I assume the premise behind the fee was it reduced her number of patients while keeping her revenue at the level it was before the move. Fewer patients meant less burnout. The same amount of revenue meant less burnout. I assume the insurance companies had beaten her down over the years and she wanted nothing to do with them anymore.

I liked her, but I didn't want to pay the fee on top of my insurance premiums and process my own claims. I figured that another doc in the group she left would take over as my PCP. I was wrong. Those other docs weren't taking on new patients. When I called to explain I wasn't a *new* patient but an *existing* patient of the group, the receptionist clarified for me that the group wasn't taking on the patients left behind by my concierge doc. So, new patient or not, there was no doc in the group who'd take care of me.

The group fired me.

The next day, I received an automated email from the group: "We would love to hear your feedback about your experience."

Seriously? You mean—how do I feel about getting fired? I ignored it.

Act One – Scene Two: A year later, I received a call from the group asking me to schedule my annual physical. I was elated. "Great. I'll have a doc assigned to me." I called and asked which doc would see me, then told none of them would. They weren't seeing any former patients of the concierge doc.

"Then why did you call asking me to schedule my annual physical?" I said.

"A nurse practitioner here will conduct your physical."

"So an NP I've not seen before will take me on as a patient, but the doc she works for won't?"

"Correct."

"And if the NP finds something wrong with me, will a doc in the group tend to me?"

"I'm not sure."

"Hmm. Okay. Thank you for your time."

The next day, I received an automated email from the group: "We would love to hear your feedback about your experience."

My Lord. I needed to get off the group's automated list.

Act Two – Scene One: We found a PCP at a nearby University of Colorado practice who was taking new patients. Three docs in this practice. My new doc was young and seemed to go on extended leaves of absence. When he was out, no one at the practice could say when he'd return. When he left, his receptionist canceled any pending appointments with a note to rebook the appointment when the doctor returned. Not ideal but . . . he was my doc.

I needed a partial knee replacement, so I needed the standard pre-op tests: EKG, blood work, urine sample, and physical. My doc was out again, so the receptionist assigned me to a different doc in the practice for the pre-ops. He wasn't impressive and he knew nothing about me, but I wasn't worried. These pre-op exams are simple, and I expected no problems. My doc would be back eventually, and we could pick up where we left off.

⁂

Act Two – Scene Two: After my knee surgery, my doc returned. I scheduled a telemed to make sure he was up to date about the surgery and to discuss and get his advice on some other conditions that had developed in his absence.

As soon as the video call began, he explained he wasn't taking new patients.

"I'm not a *new* patient at all. I'm *your* patient."

"No, you're not. When you saw the other doc, you became his patient. No longer mine."

"I only saw him because you were out for an extended leave."

"Doesn't matter. You're his patient now, and I'm not taking new ones on."

"Then I guess this video session is over?"

"Not necessarily. What additional health issues did you want to discuss?"

Bizarre. He wanted me to tell him what was wrong, and then what? Was he going to tell me he couldn't help me? I believe so. You can't make this stuff up. As I gazed at my now former doc, I imagined a skit that would go something like this:

"Doc, I came here for health advice."

"Mr. Shaiken, I can't give you health advice. I'm not your doctor. We give health advice down the hall in room 208B. This is room 208C. Here, I'll listen and nod and feign empathy."

"But I want you to be my doctor like you were before and get your advice."

"Advice is down the hall. 208B. This is 208C: listening, nodding, and feigning."

He presented as another burned-out doctor as well:

"overwhelming exhaustion, feelings of cynicism and detachment from the job, and a sense of ineffectiveness and lack of accomplishment."

Definitely detached. Definitely ineffective. Definitely nothing accomplished. He looked tired and sounded cynical. I had another burned-out thirty-something internal practitioner on my hands.

The next day—you guessed it, I received an automated message: "Tell us how we did. Click on the link to complete a quick survey."

I wondered, "Can I complete a survey and review someone who isn't my doctor?"

This time, however, I left a review of my former doc. In the review, I asked, "Whatever happened to medicine's 'do no harm' mantra?"

I hit the "submit" button and wondered if someone would get back to me. If so, I imagined that call would go something like this:

"Mr. Shaiken. This is Barry Jones. I'm not your administrator since you don't have a doc in our hospital system. But I've read your review and wanted you to know we've filed it away in the 'he has no doc' folder here. Rest assured, it will get all the attention it deserves . . . as soon as you get a doc."

Get a doc. Three little words. Of course. I called dozens of primary care physicians affiliated with different Denver hospital systems. None were taking on new patients. None. Not a one.

No one wanted me.

I pondered placing a Craigslist ad. I wrote the one above, but I didn't submit it.

༄

Act Three: I still needed a doc. I'm still old. I'm still retired. I still ache. So I had no choice. Perhaps I never did. I capitulated, and now I've paid a fee for a concierge primary care physician. Someone new and now something new for me as well. I'm now a "subscriber" of someone's services I haven't yet met (you have to pay to meet the doc).

What do I get as a subscriber? No quarterly magazine. No warm-up shirt. No seats on the blue line. No pen with his name and number on it. Just a doc I can call and book an appointment for a checkup and some advice.

I pay a fee for access. A fee so I'm not told "the doctor isn't taking new patients," even if I wasn't a new patient.

Patient—heal thyself? Stay tuned.

46

Using the Calendar to Avoid the "Look"

WHEN YOU DON'T get up and go to work for a living, there's not much difference between the days of the week. Nothing to distinguish a weekday from a weekend. In my younger working days, not knowing the day sounded like a fun way to go through life. But with the benefit of age and wisdom, I've found it's not. I've learned it's important to distinguish the days.

We all have the same seven days. Cycling over and over. Each seven making up a week. Loosely corresponding to the phases of the moon and likely dating back to the Babylonians, the Sumerian calendar, and the Book of Genesis.

When I practiced law, my calendar was full of meetings, phone calls, court appearances, depositions, trials, appointments, reminders, deadlines, and due dates. I was busy. I kept up with everything I had to do with a very simple two-part strategy. I wrote everything down on my calendar—*everything*. And I read my calendar every morning—seven days a week. *Every morning*. No exceptions. Back in the analog days, I wrote down everything in a *Daytimer*. Like the rest of the world, I shifted to my *Outlook* calendar.

Identification of days of the week was critical to the strategy's success (and to me showing up in court at the proper date and time). It was the only way I kept my law practice train chugging along on the legal tracks.

Since I looked at my calendar every morning, I always recognized the day of the week. While there wasn't too much difference between weekdays and weekends because both involved work, the days differed from each other because I had different tasks I had to do on each of the days. And weekends were special because I didn't have to shave or dress up.

When I planned out how and when I would give up the law business, I didn't count on the obvious—once I stopped, I'd no longer have as many things on my calendar. And since I'd no longer have to go to work or court, there'd be little to distinguish one day from another.

I planned and planned, and then it happened. I stopped practicing law. But I didn't plan for the calendar problem, and I lost track of the days almost immediately. Of course, in retirement, no one made me dress up. I never had to shave. Relics of my past life, but since I could decide not to shave or dress up during the week, weekends lost their distinguishing features. And almost everything I needed to do, I could do on whatever day I wanted.

Suddenly, I had complete freedom to manage my life as I wished without outside influence and interference. Something I had dreamed of for many years.

But was I ready for such freedom? Was I able to handle it? Was it a good thing? Was it good that Sundays became the same as Tuesdays? And Fridays? And every day?

I heard a fellow retiree once say with appreciation, "Every day's a weekend when you're retired."

Perhaps, but as I got into the retirement thing, I quickly found that adage unsettling. I wanted the structure provided by the days of the week. I wanted to recognize if it was a weekday or a weekend.

What Makes Me . . . Me

I needed to know. Turns out you can take the boy out of the law practice, but you can't take the law practice out of the boy.

Turns out I needed the calendar for comfort. My daily blueprint.

The fix? Get busy and write it all down on the calendar. *Everything*. Planning to clean the townhome? Write it down on the calendar. Grocery shopping—calendar. Car wash—calendar. Board meeting—calendar. Lunch—calendar. Working on a book chapter each day—calendar. Photography gigs—calendar. The Nuggets are on TV—calendar. Book appointments with me and then keep them.

Then, each morning, continuing the reliable albeit boring routine developed over decades, there was brew a pot of Pu Erh tea, read the sports section, and study the calendar. Every day. No exceptions.

I've learned that, if nothing else, continuing the calendar strategy helps me stay grounded. And I suppose it also helps me respect and honor everyone else who still has to make it to court on time or meet whatever deadline is coming. You know, respecting the rest of the world's occupants who don't have the freedom to do what they want when they want it. You know, the people who are dreaming of having nothing on their calendars.

Most importantly, keeping my calendar routine plays a very important role in helping me avoid the "look." It turns out that in retirement, I want to avoid the "look" for as long as possible. That blank stare on an aging face that says, "I'm confused." Or "I can't remember." Or "I'm just an old dude. Leave me alone." That look. You've seen it. The one that the younger set sees and says to themselves, "He's just old and can't remember."

My trusty calendar will help me remember and avoid that look.

At some point, I'll have that blank look because an ever-increasing number of things I want to remember will escape my recall. That day is coming. I get it. But I don't have to hasten that day by not understanding what day it is.

For now, I recognize what day it is. It says so right here on my calendar.

47

My Time

Kevin Durant said, "My time is now." For most of us, "now" is usually later. I've had a number of encounters with "my time" in my life and I'm not sure I'm looking forward to the next one.

When I was young, someone told me, "Kid, your time will come." He even chuckled as he elaborated it wasn't my time yet, and for emphasis, hummed the 1963 song "Our Day Will Come." I was too young to know what he meant that "my time" would come, but whatever he meant, it was clear my time hadn't come yet.

When I was a basketball player warming the bench, on the rare occasions the coach put me in, he'd look down the bench to me and say, "Shaiken. Your time." In I went for my one minute and twenty-two seconds of glory (and maybe a basket). Despite Coach's comment, that short period surely couldn't have been "my time."

In college, my advisor told me, "Mark, it's your time here at Haverford. Grab for all the gusto. Be a sponge. Soak it all in." I soaked in some of it, but I also tried not to let my education impede my education. Maybe that's what my advisor was saying. Unclear. Without knowing exactly what she meant, I'm not able to say if Haverford College was "my time" or a good time.

What Makes Me . . . Me

I toiled away as an associate at the first big law firm where I worked. As I approached partnership, the firm increased the number of years an associate had to work before partnership consideration. Law firms always reserve the right to change the rules governing associate advancement in the middle of the game. No grandfathering associates in at law firms.

My supervising partner saw my disappointment, and in an airport bar at DFW International Airport, told me, "Look. It's not a question of if. Just when." He meant well. He was trying to do the best he could with the hand the firm had dealt both of us. "It's not your time yet. It will be eventually," he explained.

I left the firm before it ever became "my time" but not because it wasn't my time yet. Life took over, and we moved away for my wife's career.

We ended up in Kansas City (Missouri, not Kansas), and I joined another big firm as a partner. It seemed I was on the cusp of it being "my time." How was I so sure it might finally be "my time" at the new Kansas City firm? Lots of trials. Lots of clients who said, "See ya in court" and put their trust in me. "My time" was this: prepare for tomorrow late into the night. Crawl home at midnight. Quick snack, PJs, kiss the kid as he slept soundly, slip into bed next to the spouse, toss and turn. Up and out at the crack of dawn for an all-day session in court. Then repeat.

This wasn't the greatest version of "my time" I could have imagined. In my new "my time," I controlled nothing. The law life swept me along in the currents of the raging Law River.

But it was "my time." Right? That's what I'd been waiting for. Wait. *That's* what I'd been waiting for?

A few chaotic decades of "my time" later, I decided it was "my time" to give up the law life and retire from the practice of law. It was time. "My time" as an attorney had become "my time" to move on.

Retirement has been great. "My time" in the sun to explore and flourish in new, untested ways.

But lately, I've wondered about the whole "my time" thing. I've realized that the next "my time" is a coda. The ending. This time, when "my time" comes, I'll cease to exist.

Some days, I hear this new, disturbing "my time" way off in the distance. If I close my eyes, I can imagine I feel it faintly.

I can't see it yet, but it's certainly out there. Yes, "my time" is coming. Without a doubt, sooner than I'd realized. But not the "my time" of my youth and my professional years. It's that last, other kind of "my time" we all encounter.

In the end, that last "my time" is a game-changer, and it always comes.

Employment & Me

48

The Bagel Bakery (The Case of the Forklift & the Rolling Bagels)

THIS STORY IS all about bagels . . . and making your way in the world. If you like bagels (and I do), please know this piece isn't about eating them. It's about them rolling around on the bakery floor.

The story begins right after I graduated from college. While I tried to figure out what I would do with life, I worked at a bagel bakery on the graveyard shift from 10 p.m. to 6 a.m., I drove a forklift, transporting skids of freshly packaged bagels into a cryogenic freezer and skids of frozen bagels out to the trucks for delivery.

It wasn't any ordinary bakery. It was the Lender's Bagel Bakery in West Haven, Connecticut, the largest frozen bagel bakery operation in North America, if not the world. It produced over a million bagels a year.

A little about bagels and Lender's before I return to my gig there.

Bagels arrived in America with the influx of Eastern European immigrants in the late nineteenth century. Harry Lender immigrated from Poland to New Haven to escape the growing wave of antisemitism and opened a fresh bagel bakery with his relatives. The boys in the family, Murray, Marvin, Sam, and Hyman, later joined the business.

For decades, bagels remained a Jewish, East Coast niche food. When Harry died in 1958, the boys took over the business and eventually, Murray and Marvin owned and ran it.

They had the audacious dream of bringing bagels to all of America. They turned to automation and converted the bakery into a bagel factory. To accommodate the proper way to make bagels (boiling and baking the dough), they developed huge commercial bagel ovens and large vats of boiling water that would automatically boil and then flip the bagels at precisely the correct moment.

The 1970s saw a dramatic rise in America's frozen food culture, and Murray and Marvin had positioned themselves to ride the wave. Bagels have a short shelf life, so the brothers added cryogenic freezers to freeze the bagels and then developed pre-slicing machines. They began shipping frozen, pre-sliced bagels nationwide to grocery stores and the bagel craze caught on.

To acclimate the masses to bagels, in one of the first Lender's marketing campaigns, they dubbed bagels the "Jewish English Muffin."

Marvin Lender said, "When we decided to make the move and do frozen, frozen foods were just coming alive." The brothers observed that Sara Lee's founder, Charles Lupin, had just released a line of frozen cheesecakes. Marvin reported, "Murray and I looked at each other and said, 'If Charlie can freeze a cheesecake, we can freeze a bagel.'"

Not everyone embraced frozen bagels. Wine critic Eric Asimov wrote in the *New York Times* that there was an "informal border" between those who ate supermarket (Lender's) bagels and those who knew better.

Despite Asimov, Lender's was so successful that in 1984, Kraft Foods bought it.

※

So where do I fit in? Remember, I was the graveyard shift guy, moving the bagels into the freezer and then out to the trucks.

But there was a problem. I was the college kid who had no previous experience driving a forklift. As fate would have it, forklifts were considerably different from my 1977 four-speed, manual transmission, dark blue Datsun B210.

I received forklift training from the nighttime supervisor, my forklift teacher. He was from South America and spoke fluent Portuguese and English but was a little hard to understand. I was the American Studies major combining American Literature and History who spoke fluent English and not a bit of Portuguese.

There was language-free, hands-on training in the forklift, to be sure, but it wasn't like the high school driving classes I had taken.

All too quickly, I graduated from the abbreviated forklift driving class and began lifting skids of bagels, delivering them to the freezer, and stacking them twelve high.

I was good at driving the forklift forward. Reverse needed practice.

Shaquille O'Neal once observed: "They shot the ball well early. But what comes out of the microwave hot doesn't always stay hot. I know because I eat bagels in the morning."

Despite needing work on the reverse gear, I was a hot commodity in this new job and liked the people I worked with, language barrier notwithstanding.

Until, like Shaq's bagels, things cooled off precipitously...

※

That fateful night, bagels rolled off the baking conveyor belt like they were supposed to; people bagged them six to a bag and deposited them in boxes, which were stacked on a nearby skid for me to do my thing.

I picked up the skid like I was supposed to and drove it into the freezer. Even though it was the heat of summer, I had my Lender's parka on because the freezer was . . . well, freezing.

And now we come to the moment when what comes out of the microwave doesn't stay hot.

I stopped next to a tower of skids ten high, deposited the new skid on the top without incident, and put the forklift into reverse to back out.

But something went terribly wrong (damn that reverse gear) and I backed the forklift into another tower of skids. The tower swayed (not a good thing in the frozen bagel world), and in slow motion, skids toppled.

The bags exploded from the impact of the fall, and frozen, pre-sliced bagels rolled everywhere. Hundreds, maybe thousands of hard, cold bagels were freed from their bags and rolling chaotically as if to escape capture. Some rolled out of the freezer and onto the bakery floor, where the evening crew worked to package bagels.

The rolling bagels quickly caught the supervisor's eye. He raced over, yelling something in Portuguese. I got the gist. His hands clutched and pulled the hair on his head. I understood the sentiment.

Someone called Marvin Lender, whom my family knew well, which is how I got the job.

It was 3:35 a.m. Within ten minutes, Marvin arrived in what appeared to be his bathrobe and began yelling. Some of it was in English. Some may have been in Yiddish. But the supervisor and I understood all of it. The supervisor explained things in Portuguese, and Marvin seemed to understand it.

Bottom line—I was the culprit.

Marvin turned to me and yelled, "What happened?!" He may've sworn. I can't remember.

As I tried to explain, I used my collegiate problem-solving skills and suggested that we could just pick up the frozen bagels and re-bag them. For certain, that would've violated every health ordinance ever issued by the city of West Haven, the state of Connecticut, and the United States.

That idea wouldn't fly, and Marvin yelled at me, "SILENCE!!!" I stopped talking mid-sentence because he was the boss and I was a loyal employee trying to drive the forklift on the graveyard shift.

※

Well, not after that night. After that night, forklift driving was just another line on my post-college resume.

Eventually, I went to law school, joined a law firm, and can say with certainty that I drove no firm forklifts or equivalents thereof.

※

There was that time, however, that I shattered the managing partner's custom-made graphite shaft golf club he had lent me to compete in the firm's annual long-drive contest.

Coming up next.

49

The Long Drive Contest

THERE WAS A point in my life when I played golf. Or at least tried to. I was terrible.

When my wife gave birth to our son in 1993, I gave up the game. I always imagined the greenskeepers of the world must have rejoiced when I retired from the game. When I played, I made their job harder. I never had golf lessons, and I tore up golf courses. I always feared they would take up a collection to pay me not to play.

Golf came into my life this way. I went to Richard C. Lee High School in New Haven, Connecticut, a very inner-city school. It had a golf team, but because of a lack of interest, anyone who wanted to play and had some clubs was on the team. I was one of those anyones.

I had a sorry collection of mismatched garage sale clubs. Our team was terrible. But we had fun. I was co-captain with Eddie N. senior year and he signed my yearbook saying he would see me soon on the pro tour.

Haha haha.

What Makes Me . . . Me

Years later, after law school classes ended each day, I went downtown, where I worked at a law firm in Topeka, Kansas, researching and writing. It was a good way to get experience. I also ran errands for the firm, using the managing partner's Mustang convertible. A fun car to drive around the Kansas capital.

I had hoped the managing partner liked me, maybe enough to make me an offer to work at the firm full-time after graduation.

Each summer, the firm had an outing for the attorneys, staff, and their families at the Topeka Country Club. It was a reasonably big shindig held on one of the golf course fairways near the clubhouse. Each year at the outing, after everyone got liquored up, the firm had a long drive contest in which any of the invited guests could take part.

I went to two of the annual outings with my wife, Loren. We're not big shindig folks, but we had a good time at the first outing, although I drank little and didn't take part in the long drive contest.

The next year, however, was quite different. By this time, I had developed a close friendship with one of the younger partners at the firm, John. He and his wife and Loren and I drank some beers together, waiting for the food tables to open. Then came the announcement. "Anyone who wants to take part in the firm's 1980 long drive contest should report to the tee."

I don't remember which Topeka Country Club hole hosted the outing in 1980, but it was one of the golf course's memorable holes: a tree-lined fairway with trees surrounding the tee box.

I didn't have a club with me; I expected to be a fan watching the others compete like the year before. But my friend John remembered I had played high school golf. He forgot the part of the story where I told him I was terrible. He encouraged me to enter the contest and convinced the managing partner to loan me his brand new, oversized head, graphite shaft, custom-made driver.

Dispensing with my freshly minted legal training, I considered none of the potential consequences of this arrangement and agreed.

That was a mistake that reminded me throughout my law career to always consider the consequences.

When my turn came, with this beautiful driver in hand, the best driver I would ever swing, I stepped onto the tee box, placed a tee in the ground, put a ball on the tee, took a couple of practice swings, and drove my ball right down the middle of the fairway. Unusual for me. Back in the day, I sprayed my shots around. Not that first shot in Topeka. Good swing, good contact, straight as an arrow shot.

On that first swing, I held back. All I wanted to do was make contact and not embarrass myself.

John applauded. The managing partner nodded and said, "Nice shot."

In the contest, each golfer got three shots. I now had a good feeling about the contest and even about my chances. I repeated the tee, ball, and practice swing ritual and stepped up for what was supposed to be my second of three shots.

Turns out it was my last shot. Number three never happened.

In the summer, Topeka, Kansas, is typically a hot and humid place. Very humid. Not as humid as Houston or New Orleans, but the air in Topeka that night was thick and wet as the summer sun started to set.

I was sweating, and I had this magnificent graphite shaft club in my sweaty hands.

I brought the club back slowly and then quickly began the downswing. My plan was to hit this shot much harder than my first and really drive the ball down the fairway. As the clubhead approached the ball, however, the club slipped out of my sweaty hands. Damn that humidity.

The onlookers quieted and watched in horror as the club flew into the woods. The only three sounds anyone heard were, in this order: first, a helicopter-like sound of the club rotating like a propeller blade as it flew: whoosh, whoosh, whoosh, whoosh; second, a nauseating and repeating booming, cracking sound as the club reached the woods and crashed from tree trunk to tree trunk: Boom,

boom, boom, boom; and third, "Motherfucker" uttered slowly by the managing partner, who emphasized each syllable, making no effort to speak his mind under his breath.

John ran to the woods and retrieved some pieces of the club. I guess that was all he could think of doing. No one ever found the rest of the pieces. No one tried. Why would they?

I wanted to say I was sorry and offer to buy a new club, but John said the managing partner was too mad and needed time to cool off.

The next day at work, I knocked on the managing partner's door and he grunted in what sounded like permission to enter. I said as sincerely as I could how sorry I was and offered to buy him a new club. He looked down at his desk and gruffly said, "Not necessary." No eye contact. Always a bad sign. Also, I didn't have the money to buy that new custom-made club for him, especially at the hourly wages he paid me. He knew that.

Soon after, my role of running errands for the firm in that very cool Mustang convertible owned by the managing partner also ended. I guess he was worried I would drive the car into the woods as well. Also a bad sign.

Later in the school year, as I neared graduation, John asked me if I would apply to be a full-time attorney at the firm. I wanted to, but I was worried the managing partner would reject the application based on the unfortunate long-drive contest results. John acted confident it wouldn't be a factor. So I applied.

Weeks later, after class, I arrived at the office, and the receptionist told me the managing partner wanted to see me in his office. She and I had gotten along great during my time at the firm, but she made no eye contact with me when she delivered the message. Another bad sign.

I went down the hall to the managing partner's office, trying hard not to jam my hands deep into my pockets as I walked. I arrived at his door, knocked, and without looking up, he waved me in.

He didn't tell me to sit, so I stood. He looked up. A

classic, time-tested technique to make the subordinate even more uncomfortable.

"We've decided we're not going to be able to make you an offer to join the firm after you graduate."

No question was asked, so I said nothing. He grunted and continued. "I just wanted you to know this is an economic decision and has nothing to do with the golf club thing."

Golf club *thing*? I frowned imperceptibly. It wasn't a "thing." It was just short of an international incident with sanctions against me to be taken up by the United Nations Security Council.

I asked him if he wanted me to leave the firm before graduation. He said that wasn't necessary. I thanked him (not sure for what) and headed back to my desk to research, write, and ponder.

John later said the decision had nothing to do with the golf club *thing*. There was that "thing" word again.

The U.N. Security Council never took up the matter. It didn't need to. Sanctions had already been imposed. I'm sure the Council members saw it as just another one of those "oh well" moments we all go through as we try to make our way through life. I'm sure the Council members unanimously concluded I should never have entered the long drive contest.

50

The Aptitude Test

I WENT TO law school over forty-five years ago. Before that, I wandered from one career path idea to the next until the walls of maturity closed in on me and I heard the call of needing money for food and rent.

But, even as those walls pressed closer to me, I still didn't know what to do with my life, what career might suit me, what I might enjoy doing.

I had driven a forklift—not well. I had painted lines on state highways—mine were the crooked ones. I had been a septic tank troubleshooter (need I say more?). I had made sandwiches, waited tables, mowed lawns, made copies in an office, and I had sampled many other endeavors. Nothing wrong with any of them, but none excited me or suited my fancy.

So I took a career aptitude test, administered in an office by a professional career counselor.

I figured the test would tell me what I should do in my life. It would identify my strengths and interests.

I promised to answer the questions honestly and to the best of my ability. The instructions told me not to worry whether I knew how to perform the tasks or how much money I might make in a related career. The test asked me to focus on whether I thought I'd enjoy doing the task.

The introduction told me there were no right or wrong answers.

For each task, the test asked me to rank my likes and dislikes on a scale of one to five. The test portrayed a "one" as a frowning face and a "five" as an ecstatic face.

One to five. Frowning. Happy. I got it.

I took the test and ranked my likes and dislikes for things like roof and air conditioning repair, plumbing, electrical work, nuclear energy, math, reviewing financial records, politics, reading, writing, drawing, teaching, driving, and many other things.

I rated most of the tasks right in the middle: solid twos and threes. Total ambivalence. So many things I neither liked nor disliked. I gave out a single five for writing.

The professional scheduled a follow-up meeting, and we met in a room laid out much like a psychologist's room with a desk, chairs, and a couch. I avoided the couch.

Sitting at her desk across from me, she came right to the point. "This says you want to be a writer." She said it with disbelief and a small measure of disdain that she didn't hide. Perhaps she had called my father and talked to him before the session with me. Who knows; all I could do was smile. She frowned. "You promised to answer the questions honestly and to the best of your ability," she said.

"I did, and I did."

She shook her head. She narrowed her eyes and said, "I don't think so."

I shook my head. "But the instructions said there were no right or wrong answers."

No response. She looked down at her desk and, with that slight movement, ended the meeting and dispatched me into the world to figure it all out on my own without the skill set necessary to do so.

It was a short meeting. Apparently, I had evidenced no aptitude

What Makes Me . . . Me

for any career. No goodbyes. No *thank yous*. No *good lucks*. I just left. No follow-up report from her. I don't remember if there was an attorney question on the failed aptitude test. If there was, I'm sure I would have rated it a two.

Yet, without knowing if I had any aptitude to be an attorney or interest in such a career, for that matter, I decided to give law school a go and allow myself three more years to figure it all out. As I arrived at the front doors to the law school and the gateway to the rest of my life and my career by default, some things were apparent.

One—I told myself as I began the rest of my life that I'd attend law school just until I figured out what I would do. I never intended to be an attorney and have a law practice, let alone go to court for clients (bankruptcy court for me) for the four decades that followed.

Two—I was sure I must have had some aptitude for something. Or at least as sure as any twenty-two-year-old could be. I would just have to figure out what that might be (it turns out, for me, it was the attorney gig, along with writing, photography, and music).

Three—I realized I had become the first person in the modern era, maybe in any era, to flunk an aptitude test. At least that was my takeaway from the short meeting with the professional.

Crazy test. Crazy process. Crazy professional. Crazy result, at least according to the professional.

But I've always worried: if the test results were crazy, did that mean I was crazy as well? Maybe so. Perhaps you need to be a lot crazy to go to law school. And maybe you need to be a little crazy to be a writer.

51

Work, Sleep, and Repeat

I FOUND COMFORT, even solace, in my legal practice, the earn-a-living routine of work, sleep, and repeat. But it wasn't always like that.

I had an acquaintance in high school whose father owned a local record store near the Yale campus. The best record store in Connecticut, in my estimation. His routine was his father's. He showed up at the record store and did whatever was necessary to attend to customers and stock and sell the records. Later in life, the store became his.

My dad didn't own a record store. While he earned a living and went off to work each morning, I wasn't part of his routine, so I had to learn my own and try to find my comfort and solace. The work, sleep, and repeat routine represented job responsibility, but I didn't learn it early on. I was a terribly slow learner, starting off my working life with a devil-may-care attitude of coming to work late or skipping a day, sometimes with consequences.

Consequences are always a good way to teach lessons. As I learned to find the routine, I even learned some life lessons along the way.

What Makes Me . . . Me

I had my first paying job when I was thirteen. A friend of mine and I mowed lawns in the summer for the people with the big houses and even bigger lawns. Because we had no driver's licenses, we could only mow the lawns that we could walk to in the streets with our mowers.

Some homeowners wanted their lawns mowed late in the day. Perfect for a thirteen-year-old hoping to sleep in over the summer. Some wanted their lawns mowed first thing in the morning. Not so perfect.

I don't remember how many times I missed the eight a.m. whistle. Surprisingly, my friend never got mad. He was an early riser and didn't miss any appointments, so when I didn't show, he mowed the whole lawn and pocketed the entire fee.

I was young and more than just a little irresponsible. And I liked my shut-eye. But I learned at thirteen that no one pays you for sleeping in. And I needed the money. So, I also learned how to roll my bones out of bed no matter how sleepy I was.

My next summer job was as an athletic counselor at the junior high across the street. All I had to do was show up and play basketball with the ten-year-old day campers who wanted to play. Very few showed up to the gym. It was a hot summer, and the gym lacked air conditioning. As they failed to show up, I came to work a little later and then a little later than that. One day, a camp supervisor came by when I was good enough to show up and chewed me out, making sure to tell me how lucky I was to have a job. I didn't enjoy getting yelled at, but he was right, so after the yelling, I came on time every day. I used the empty gym time to practice. Turns out, if I considered the requirement to be on time as an appointment to play basketball, I showed up. If I saw it as a job requirement, I was less reliable.

Note to self: think of work as fun if at all possible (I later abandoned this notion during one of my bankruptcy court trials).

There was the late-night sub shop job of making sandwiches for the recently inebriated. By this point, I had learned how to get to work on time, punch in, and wait for my shift to end. More progress for me.

What else did I learn at the sandwich gig? How to clean up after the recently inebriated who had no business eating a mayonnaise-laden, double tuna sandwich after midnight. Apparently, their bodies agreed.

I re-visited the sandwich experience years later as I considered the stress of my law job. I concluded that the law job was much less stressful and so much more sanitary than cleaning up after tuna drunks.

One summer, I painted lines on the state highways. I had no car, so I rode my bike to work, and by then, I had learned to arrive at work on time. There wasn't much on-the-job training, and I didn't have any artistic talent. I painted my lines crooked, and my supervisor relegated me to walking behind the line painter and dumping little glass beads into the wet paint so that at night, the lines would glow in the reflection of a car's headlights.

My co-worker had spent the summer admonishing me not to turn out like him and stay in college. He even nicknamed me "College Boy," which might seem pejorative, but he didn't mean it that way. I quit the job before the summer ended to get a head start on my junior year in college and eliminate any doubt about my intentions of staying in school.

I reflected on my painting job from time to time as the law years rolled by. Not wistfully. Just from a historical perspective. To every season, turn, turn, turn. Can't know where you're going until you know where you've been.

I repaired mobile home park septic tank hookups one summer. I always arrived on time. I always left on time at the end of the day.

Nasty, stinky work. Especially when I had to hop down into the hole my supervisor had dug to make an initial assessment of the problem. Often, my assessment was simple, as I yelled up to the supervisor, "Yep. She's definitely clogged!"

Brilliant.

I've learned that hardship often breeds brilliance. And make no mistake. I found it an extreme hardship to be standing in inches of septic water—the same as sewer water—filled with, well, you can imagine, wearing my faithful Converse sneakers and Lee jeans. I stunk. The water stunk. The hole stunk. The job stunk. The homeowner who flushed whatever shouldn't have been flushed also stunk. Easy to see how I might conclude the world stunk that summer.

I didn't recall my septic tank hookup job much during the practice of law. Sure, I might conclude the occasional case I had stunk. But "stunk" is all relative. Nothing in court could possibly compare to septic tank hookup repair work.

Our experiences make us who we are. I learned not to expect to sleep in. I learned that to be paid, I had to show up each day, physically and mentally. I came to find comfort in reliably arriving at the law firm each day. I came to appreciate that I was able to do some things in life better than others. I came to accept that while the practice of law was hard, there were many harder ways to go through life and make a living.

The *3J Legal Thriller* Series

52

You Go Girl: The Story of 3J and Her Series

IN MY LEGAL and financial thriller series, my protagonist is Josephina Jillian Jones, 3J to her friends. She's a Black female bankruptcy law partner in a large Kansas City law firm. I'm neither Black nor female.

Here's a little about what she's like and the answers to some questions about her and the series.

When you write fiction, you get to create your own little galaxy. 3J is the empress of my galaxy. She's the hazel-eyed kid from New Orleans's Lower Ninth Ward and Tremé who took the education train out of the Crescent City but not the graduation train back.

She went to Whitman College (in Walla Walla, Washington) and Washburn University School of Law (in Topeka, Kansas, like me).

For a time, she was the only female Black partner at her large (fictional) law firm, Greene Madison, located high atop downtown Kansas City, Missouri, at 1201 Walnut Street, overlooking the Power & Light District (like my old law firm).

[I include Missouri in the location because there's also a Kansas City, Kansas, across the river, and so many people mistakenly assume the main part of Kansas City, where the Chiefs and Royals play, is in Kansas. It's not.]

She loves jazz and barbecue (like me). She's tenacious in the defense of her clients (I hope my clients felt that I was).

She worries that the practice of law is impeding her ability to stay fit. She laments that she had a six-pack in college, a four-pack and then a two-pack in law school, and now a no-pack in the practice of law.

You can meet her here.

She often runs toward danger. Her father tried to teach her not to and worried she wasn't learning the lesson. He died months before Katrina made landfall, but now her law firm mentor and friend, William Pascale, and her boyfriend, Ronnie Steele, have taken over her father's job of worrying.

When she suggests she should take on noted Irish mobster Robbie McFadden, her friends instantly shoot her down, and she later insists to Steele that she was just kidding. But everyone knows she isn't.

Some questions about the series and the answers.

Why a Black woman? Several reasons. First, I'm mindful that I don't and couldn't feel what it's like to be a Black woman in a largely White male Midwestern law firm. I've observed the struggle and I hate that there is a struggle, but I haven't, and couldn't, live it. But if I only created characters who looked like me—an older, graying, white male—all my characters would be homogenous and wouldn't reflect the world I live in. I want my books to reflect my world. It's important to me to have characters from different walks of life—like 3J.

Second, having a strong Black female protagonist like 3J gives me the chance to address things in the world I don't like. Things like racial discrimination, White Nationalism and hate, mental illness, redlining in housing, greed, and felonious conduct. 3J represents her clients zealously and sets out to right such wrongs.

Third, 3J is flawed, like me, like all of us. I don't want perfect characters because I'm not perfect, and I don't know anyone who is. I want conflicted, sometimes unpredictable characters: bad good guys, good bad guys, and, of course, bad bad guys.

Do I like 3J? I do. I'd love to grab a cup of coffee or have lunch with her someday. Until then, I get to talk to her aloud when I'm writing to make sure my dialogue is genuine.

Why set the stories in Kansas City, Missouri? We lived there for over twenty-five years. You write what you know. And it's a wonderful place. For all you flyover folks, drop in sometime. You won't be sorry.

Why jazz? I love it, and Kansas City was such an important part of the growth of jazz in the United States (the Ken Burns series, as good as it was, didn't give Kansas City its due).

I worry about offering a list for fear of excluding someone, but here goes: Kansas City jazz luminaries include Count Basie; Charlie Parker (born there and played there until he headed to New York); Jay McShann (in whose big band Parker played); Ben Webster; Benny Moten; Lester Young; Mary Lou Williams; Pat Metheny; Coleman Hawkins (from St. Joseph, Missouri, just up the river from Kansas City); Andy Kirk and his Clouds of Joy; Claude "Fiddler" Williams; Bobby Watson; and Kevin Mahogany.

The city oozed music. A book set in Kansas City has to include the music.

Why references to history? Kansas City was an important part of American history, and in particular, the Civil War. Missouri was a slave state. Kansas was a free state. The Kansas City metropolitan area sits in both states. Free State and pro-slavery factions battled on the border years before the Civil War started. In many respects, the Civil War broke out on the Kansas and Missouri border years before the South seceded from the Union.

The South's loss at the battle of Westport (now a bar district in the city) was integral to the downfall of the South and Lee's surrender at Appomattox.

There's a cemetery south of downtown Kansas City named Union Cemetery. Those in charge of the Civil War dead buried

Union and Confederate soldiers there. Sometimes, side by side. Possibly the first time the two could find common ground—their shared eternal resting place.

Why the tradition of drinking at O'Brien's on Fridays? O'Brien's is a fictional bar and grill, but it's at the same corner—Pennsylvania and Westport Road—as Kelly's, an actual bar and grill.

That location was a general store before 1865 and auctioned slaves from the basement. More history that's such an iconic part of Kansas City. I imagined it would be a wonderful place for 3J and Pascale to put a period, and sometimes an exclamation point, at the end of another week in the bankruptcy trenches.

When she walks into the bar, heads turn to watch her. She knows it.

He drinks Kansas wheat beer; she drinks Irish Whiskey neat. As she would say with a smile, she could ask for it with ice, but why would she?

Why is there always a scene at a barbecue restaurant? Each book features a different famous Kansas City barbecue joint. It gives me a chance to tout the very best barbecue in the country and the smoking skills of my favorite smoke masters. Only my opinion. Sorry, Texas and Memphis.

Why a mobster character? Kansas City was a stronghold for the mob for decades until a war broke out among mob factions in the 1970s. The mob is still there, but it's more discreet. My Irish mobster, Robbie McFadden, went to Wharton. He likes to say it's just business. *Cram Down* is the first book in which McFadden appears. People die in *Cram Down*. I kind of enjoyed the writing process of killing them off.

Finally, why fiction? Turns out I like to tell stories. Not all that different from performing in bankruptcy court over the years, except those stories were true (or at least they were supposed to be). 3J tells a good tale at the courtroom podium, and Judge Robertson respects her. Hopefully, the judges I appeared before felt the same about me.

53

One Foot in Front of the Other—William Pascale

Now that you've met and read a little about 3J, what about her law mentor, William Pascale, a partner at the Greene Madison law firm?

He's a White, Western Kansas farm kid and former baseball pitcher at Kansas State University who ran into arm trouble, gave up the game, and went to law school instead. He was religious but no longer is.

He's been at the firm for decades, practicing in the Kansas City firm's headquarters at the corner of 12th and Walnut Street in downtown Kansas City, Missouri, close to where Charlie Parker exploded onto the jazz scene in the 1930s.

He hired 3J out of law school to work in the law firm's bankruptcy group. He taught her the law, trained her to be an attorney at a big firm, and then set her free to become the best possible version of herself.

He's got thinning hair and can't figure out if it's time to move into the next season of his life. He's worried that if he leaves the firm, he won't learn how to fill his days. So he stays. Most recently, he signed a one-year deal with the firm to "consult." He's the first partner-turned-consultant in the firm. Neither he nor the firm knows what it means to "consult." As he "consults," he concludes his work day hasn't changed. Rather, he just gets paid less for doing the same thing.

He and 3J meet at O'Brien's Bar on most Fridays after work to talk about their cases. The two work on many cases together, and he provides her a sounding board and a moral compass when needed.

He's had tragedy in his life: his wife and daughter died in a car crash at the hands of a drunk driver. But he perseveres, getting up each morning in his big, lonely Loose Park house, and against great odds, putting one foot in front of the other, practices law and waits for a sign, any sign, that his life will get back to normal. He wonders if the sign will ever come.

He plays acoustic and electric guitar and calls his Martin D28 acoustic his girlfriend.

⁂

So what part of the recesses of my mind did Pascale come from?

I'm not always sure where any of my characters come from. Many of them have some of my traits but all of them have traits that have nothing to do with me.

Some similar traits: Pascale, 3J, and Jacob Steinert practice bankruptcy law. They have clients. They go to court. They live and practice law in Kansas City. The law consumes most of their life.

They like some of the things I like. In no particular order: Jazz. Soccer. Barbecue. Kansas City beef. Pulled Pork. Whiskey. Guitar. Wheat beer. Loose Park. New Orleans. Washburn University. Sonos. Westport. The Chiefs. Living in Kansas City. History. Any food cooked or bourbon curated by Celina Tio.

In Pascale's case, he's older. He teaches the bankruptcy code to the young, up-and-coming attorneys in the firm. He writes songs. He sings better than me (it's fiction, so I can make his voice better than mine), and he's not afraid to get on stage on open mic night and preview a new song (I am). His songs are my songs, and when he tells 3J over a barbecue lunch that he's finished a song, that's the song that I've finished and recorded. So lots of me is in the Pascale character.

Pascale struggles (like I did) with how to exit the practice of law, and when he tries to explain his rationale and feelings to 3J, much of that is borne out of my own experiences. Many of his views about the practice of law are mine.

The one foot in front of the other moniker is me and my life, and that is Pascale's enduring quality. My wife and I have had difficult family times over the years, and the only way to get out of bed and go to work and live our lives was one day at a time, one foot in front of the other.

The traits that are similar stem from the adage: you write what you know.

Some differences: despite our family difficulties, we've had no tragedy approaching what Pascale lost the night of the fateful car crash.

Other differences: I never pitched. I never played division one baseball at a major university like Kansas State University, although my wife and I lived in Manhattan, Kansas, for a while during her veterinary school days. We never lived in a big house near Loose Park in Kansas City, but friends of ours did. I didn't grow up on a farm. I'm not from Western Kansas, although my wife is and I've spent a good amount of time there.

Pascale's office is a mess—papers everywhere. Mine was quite neat, although I had colleagues who had papers piled in their offices, forming pyramids just like Pascale. And despite that, they always seemed to find whatever they needed in the mess.

Interviewers and friends have asked me if Pascale was actually me. None of the characters are me or anyone else I know, for that matter. There are just parts of me in each character. Pascale is like most of my characters—there's some of me in them, but none are me.

That formula gives me the chance to reach inside and grab something about me and write what I know, while I can create fictional characters from things I've reflected on or dreamed about or seen or heard.

Pascale came from the same place that all of my characters come from: a little bit of me and a lot of my imagination.

What's next for Pascale? Like me, before I left the law, a new client or two and more hand-wringing, as he tries to wrestle with the eternal problem of when to leave a profession that's been his life for many decades. More music, except, unlike me, 3J will finally hear him perform.

A love interest? More sage advice for 3J? An uncomfortable meet and greet with Robbie McFadden, the Irish mobster?

And maybe none of the above. The 3J galaxy is mine to create, alter, amend, and rule. My imagination is fickle and subject to change. That's the station in life of any fiction writer. The ruler of all that I can close my eyes and see from an imaginary throne in front of a computer screen. It's no different for Pascale.

He's mine to control from the throne. It's a fun throne to occupy.

Poetry & Me

54

A Little Poetry Context

> *"Poetry is the spontaneous overflow of powerful feelings: it takes its origin from emotion recollected in tranquility."*
> – William Wordsworth.

NOT ALL MY emotions have been tranquil ones. But much of my poetry is. I started writing poems when I was in grade school. Sadly, many of them, in my handwriting, seemed to have gone to the same watery grave as many of my print photographs during the alleged flood of the 1970s (*see* "Color Confusion" Chapter 5). No matter. I don't write poems often, and when I do, I don't write them for others. I write them for myself.

A poem happens "when an emotion has found its thought and the thought has found words" – *Robert Frost*.

It would be hard to argue with Robert Frost. I like his definition.

Over the last decade, the poems I've written are the precursor to the songs I wrote. In *AJLT*, I published two poems that led to songs. I enjoyed doing that. Suddenly, I shared something that I hadn't before—my overflow of feelings for people to read.

I still write songs, which means I still write poems. Here are three more songs that started off as poems.

55

Blue Sky Afternoon

When you play music, you get to dream and immerse yourself in a different world. It's a good thing. A wonderful thing. The best thing in the world.

One thing I can dream about is what it would have been like if Bruce Springsteen had called and asked me to join the E Street Band on tour. Now that would be a moment, eh?

Rest easy. Bruce has never called me, and despite some things we hold in common, I'm sure he won't. He has all the lead guitarists he needs in his band and stocked his Rolodex with cards of other brilliant guitarists to fill in when needed.

I'm guessing there's no Mark Shaiken card to which he can flip.

But I still write my songs and play my guitar because it simply makes me very happy. Usually, the words come first. Once I have the words, I can strum out a tune. The songs without the music are my poems. Here are a few. In this first one, you can easily figure out what part of my life it's about. If you'd like to hear it (it's a jazzy number), go here.

Blue Sky Afternoon

Look out
for the clouds today.
Don't let them
come my way.
They only make
the sky so gray.
Please send those
clouds away.

Just smile
and they'll retreat.
Then you and I can meet.
On a blue sky
afternoon.

I've looked both
near and far.
East of the moon.
West of the stars.
Gazed at *Umbrellas*
by Renoir.
Then I realized
well, here we are.

Just smile
and repeat
when you and I can meet
On a blue sky
afternoon.

Let's meet by the carousel
and take that ride we know so well.

Let's stroll by the ice cream man
and share the day,
hand in hand.

I feel the love
and so do you.
A crazy kind
of love for two.
Our souls,
they speak the truth.
And when they do,
there's no dispute.

Just smile
love's complete
when you and I can meet.
It's a blue sky,
Afternoon.
Blue sky
Sunday afternoon.
Just a blue sky
afternoon.

Don't Ever Change

Here's the second one. I got to record this one with Colorado Sound's Steve Avedis at his home recording and engineering studio in Lakewood, Colorado. Thanks to Steve for making me sound better than I am. If you'd like to hear it, go here.

Don't Ever Change

I will adore you.
I won't ignore you.

And so I say,
in my simple way:
I love you.

Lavender moonbeams
shine down
on such tranquil dreams.

And so I say,
in my simple way:
I love you.

Don't ever change.
Don't change at all.
Don't ever change.

Mark Shaiken

Not now.
Not ever.
Not at all.

Jupiter flies
and twinkling stars scoot by.
The man in the moon
hustles home,
to see you
soon.

Mountain sunrise
turns into all those times

when I can say,
in my simple way:
I love you.

Don't ever change.
Don't change at all.
Don't ever change.
Not now.
Not ever.

Close your eyes dear,
and dream
when I'm not near

of the day I'll say,
in my simple way,
I love you.

Emily M'Love

FOR THE BEATLES' *White Album*, Paul McCartney wrote "Martha My Dear," a song about his sheepdog, a breed he admired based on the dog in the Dulux paint commercials that ran in Britain. In his song, Martha the Dog sort of morphs into Martha the Person. I always felt it was so cool to write songs about almost anything, as McCartney could, including his dog Martha.

Finally, I came up with a song about our little rescue dog, Emily, inspired by Sir Paul. In my song, Emily might be a person or a dog, just like in "Martha My Dear." Whether a person or a dog, Emily's a most amazing friend (Emily also has recurring cameo appearances in the 3J series).

Here's the poem that kicked off the song which ended up with a Latin beat, some jazzy chord changes, and some folk mixed in. You can listen to the song here: *https://youtu.be/gbGLN8MVMjY*.

Emily M'Love

Soft brown eyes,
gazing lovingly.
Cuddle with me now,
my sweet
Emily.

Emily m'love,
you make my life complete.

No matter what may ever pass,
I'm glad we came to meet.

Don't you worry 'bout a thing,
don't concern yourself for me.
Life's much better
when we're together,
Emily.

Share with me your world,
and I'll give you love for free.
Play with me this morning,
my lovin'
Emily.

I think I know
how much you care for me.
And while I may not always tell you,
I love you,
Emily.

Don't you worry 'bout a thing,
don't concern yourself for me.
Life's much better
when we're together,
Emily.

Lay your head
right here next to me.
Nighttime is the alright time,
my sweetie,
Emily.

Try to catch some raindrops

And bring them here to me.
Kiss me like that lollipop,
my honey,
Emily.

Don't you worry 'bout a thing,
Don't concern yourself for me.
Life's much better,
When we're together,
Emily.
Emily.
Emily.

Some More of the Law & Me

56

Once Upon a Time, I Was an Attorney

IF YOU'VE READ And Just Like That, *you know some of how the law story ended for me. Four decades, then one day, no more law . . . just like that.*

Here's a little of how it ended in AJLT, and then a little more since then.

I was an attorney for a good long time. Four decades and four-plus years ago, I went to court for the last time, said goodnight to my legal assistant for the last time, and rode the elevator down twenty-four stories for the last time. I exited our building onto Denver's 16th Street Mall and into whatever would come next.

So, now I'm not an attorney. When asked, "Who are you?" I no longer respond by saying, "I'm an attorney." And that was never "who I was" anyway. That was always just "what I did."

People ask me to talk about how I came to be an attorney and how I moved on. They sound like they're looking for advice. But I'm not qualified to tell the world how to decide to become an attorney, how to be an attorney, or how to stop being an attorney. There are many such books for sale, and I've consumed more than a few of those in my decades as a practicing attorney. I just don't find myself skilled enough to advise anyone to be—or avoid being—an attorney. I also challenge the notion that there's cookie-cutter, one-size-fits-all advice to give on those topics. What to do with a life and when to move on to try something new are very personal decisions, different for each of us, and don't lend themselves to convenient or useful rules of thumb.

I can just report the facts. Here are several.

Like so many things in my life, becoming the attorney thing just sort of happened. One day, I went to college, graduated, needed money, drove a forklift for a while, and the next day, I found myself in law school. And the next day, I passed the bar exam and began life as an attorney at law. Just like that. Well, maybe not quite the very next day, but after all the years of practicing bankruptcy law, time and space can sometimes get a little distorted and the continuum of the dimensions can warp.

Did I enjoy being an attorney? Not always. Sometimes I hated it and the law firm world, sometimes I tolerated it, and sometimes I may have even liked it. But mostly, as is true for so many attorneys, "like" was not typically the first word that crossed my mind when I pondered each day of my law life. I liked my life as an attorney more when I learned to accept the parts of the practice of law that drove me crazy and that I couldn't change. For that, I can thank life as an attorney for helping me learn I can't control everything and, at times, I can't control anything.

The practice of law frustrated me, and then, without warning, it energized me. Often, I made the people close to me miserable, and I attribute that unfortunate truth to the practice of law rather than to myself, although I can see how that's debatable. I sometimes frustrated my partners in the law firm, although . . . they may have occasionally enjoyed having me around, just a little . . . but they don't have to admit it.

Now, four years removed, I realize I didn't always—perhaps even rarely—hate the practice of law. But, on balance, "like" was and still is a hard word for me to use near the phrase "practice of law."

Most importantly, I enjoyed my colleagues at the firm, my clients, and the judges before whom I practiced. All tolerated me, and some even enjoyed having me around. I keep in touch with some of them and enjoy our get-togethers. I especially enjoy the get-togethers with colleagues where we talk about things other than the firm, the latest cases they have, and the latest rulings from around the country. Law stuff—not me anymore.

Even when I was practicing law, I liked to dream. Maybe, I needed to dream. To dream: the transitive verb, to think of the possibilities. For me, back then, this included possibilities other than a life in the law. But when the law got in the way of dreaming, I treated the law as a person like others who had named it the "jealous mistress." This mistress tried to leave me without enough time to dream. When I did dream, it resisted me and fought me.

In my years of working in law firms, as I reserved the right to seek greener pastures, I saw things, experienced things, laughed at things, cried at things, loved things, despised things, became resigned to things, and tried to set aside time to dream of other things besides trying cases in bankruptcy court.

Life as an attorney taught me to enjoy being busy, so in my law afterlife, I'm busy, but I no longer give out legal advice, write briefs, go to court, make oral arguments, call witnesses to the stand, cross-examine witnesses, and deal with my law partners on a day-to-day basis. But I don't feel like I retired. Every day, I get deeper into *My Life 2.0*.

In this new version, I choose to do many other things. For example, I smile a great deal. I swear less. I spent much of my law life not making the world a better place. Now, I try to make the world a better place, little by little, day by day, person by person, project by project, cause by cause, and I hope I'm making up for lost time. As Vincent Van Gogh said, "I would rather die of passion than of boredom." In my law life, while I wasn't bored, I lacked passion, or at least if I had it, I lost it. Now I have passion, and there's no boredom in my afterlife. The afterlife is a good deal for me . . . so far.

And that afterlife? I've pivoted to a life of writing books—five since I hung up the wingtips. This is number six. You can find them on Amazon and other booksellers as well as at the end of this book in my "library." Apart from the memoir and these essays, you write what you know. So, my other books are fiction—legal and financial thrillers.

Many days are taken up with not-for-profit service. Every day is taken up with music (I'm not great, but I love it). I'm even taking singing lessons now. I'm a real project. I don't expect to sound like Tony Bennett anytime soon, but it's fun and I look forward to the get-togethers with my teacher.

Some weeks are taken up with travel. I was never a world traveler, and it's an enormous world. So far, United gets us where we want to go in one piece. I'm grateful for that.

Even in *My Life 2.0*, I allow myself to ruminate about my journey away from the law life. You can't know where you're going unless you know where you've been.

It took me a long time to learn this about my years as an attorney: while there may be better ways to go through life, there are many, many worse ways to go through life. Really.

At some point, however, it's time to part ways. And for me, it was time to move on. Turns out it was a good decision for me.

57

Teaching Law—What Was I Thinking?

I TAUGHT BANKRUPTCY law at the University of Kansas Law School for fourteen years. I was an adjunct professor, and this was my second job as I also practiced law at my large law firm. They were wonderful years. My legal administrative assistant noted that on the days I taught, I had a big smile on my face when I returned to the law office.

After the first class, the experience of teaching at KU was both memorable and rewarding. Oh, but that first class was a doozy.

I was so honored when KU asked me to teach that I failed to figure out why I wanted to.

Bankruptcy was an early morning class populated by law school seniors—3Ls. I settled in on a routine. I'd get to Lawrence, Kansas, at about 7 a.m., stop at Dunkin' Donuts for a coffee and a chocolate glazed donut, and go over my class lesson before heading over to the law school.

I started teaching at KU with little to no idea what I was getting myself into. That first Monday morning, before the donut routine settled in, I arrived at the law school and headed for the professorial coffee urn in a room next to the dean's office.

I had always heard about the urn but had never been in the urn room because I had never been a professor.

There, I found full-time, tenured professors caffeinating themselves and exchanging war stories before class or talking about KU's legendary basketball team. I was just an adjunct. I said little that first morning, taking it all in.

It was a privilege to be in that little room drinking the dean's coffee and listening to people who had taught law for decades, many of whom were icons in the law business. It was the law equivalent of being in the locker room as Nicola Jokić and his Denver Nuggets teammates suited up and prepared for their next NBA basketball game.

Then, at 7:50, I headed for the classroom to set up and greet the students—sixty-four of them—to begin our semester-long journey together through the bankruptcy code and the law of debtor-creditor relations.

Until that moment, I hadn't been nervous. I knew more than they did about bankruptcy law, or at least I took comfort in thinking that I did. I wasn't a poor speaker. I went to law school, and I was well acquainted with what was supposed to happen in a law school class.

What could go wrong?

The students were prompt, and at 8 a.m., I stepped in front of the podium. I introduced myself. I looked out at the sea of soon-to-be new attorneys, all focused on graduating and passing the bar exam.

And . . . then it happened.

I had my first and only out-of-body experience. As I heard myself speak, a part of me seemed to rise out of my body and hover above. The *hovering me* observed the *speaking me* addressing the students, who were listening intently. From that vantage point, the *hovering me* wondered: "What in heaven's name am I doing? Why did I assume I could teach, let alone teach law school?"

The *speaking me* voice quavered, "Good morning. I'm Mark Shaiken and will teach Bankruptcy 101 this semester. I've practiced bankruptcy law for . . . " blah, blah, blah.

The *hovering me* reflected on the problem that my voice didn't quaver when I went to court. It didn't quaver when I cross-examined a witness. It didn't quaver when I addressed a judge or a panel of judges, all of whom had the power to stop me from speaking merely by raising their hands like a traffic cop stopping traffic. But here, in front of sixty-four people with no obvious power to stop me from speaking, I conveyed nervousness, which provided a sense that I lacked confidence.

"My lord," the *hovering me* said silently. If the *speaking me* couldn't confidently explain who I was, what was going to happen for the rest of the semester?

The *hovering me* and the *speaking me* determined in unison: not a good way to start a law school class. Not a good look for students paying so much money to attend law school.

Despite both the *speaking me* and *hovering me*, that first class went fine, or as fine as any first day of law school class could be. At least I felt it did.

But I was rattled.

⚜

After that first class, I turned to the question I should have addressed before accepting the KU offer to teach: why did I want to teach? I should have answered that question before I accepted the offer to teach and, at the very least, before the first class. But I hadn't, and it was time to do so.

My deliberation was a quick one. I had plenty of work back at the firm. I didn't need a second job. Maybe it was because I wanted to do something where people saw me. Sixty-four students. But that made little sense. I went to court all the time. People saw me there. I worked in a large law firm. Colleagues saw me there. I had lots of clients. They saw me regularly.

I decided it was because I enjoyed helping smart people "get it." Bankruptcy law was hard to get. Turns out I wanted to be the sherpa who led them around the Bankruptcy Code as their law guide. I had helped young associates assigned to our bankruptcy group "get it" and found that was my favorite part of the job. That was a one-on-one experience. How cool would it be to guide sixty-four soon-to-be law firm associates around the Code? Very cool, I decided.

With that figured out, I hoped for a little more confidence and no more out-of-body experiences in class number two and beyond.

※

Wednesday rolled around. Class No. 2. Same protocol. I arrived at the dean's office for my second experience at the coffee urn. My second professorial cup of coffee with the other, much more experienced professors who gathered around the urn and talked. This time, I was nervous. All I could think about was avoiding any further out-of-body experiences.

My funk ended when one of my longtime mentors in the stable of professors invited me into the conversation.

"Well, Professor Shaiken. How did day one of your budding teaching career go?" Professor Clark asked.

All of his professor buddies stopped talking and turned to watch me answer. I nearly choked on my coffee. I mustered a weak smile and said, "Not so great. Actually, I wondered why in hell I presumed I could ever teach these folks anything. I wondered why they would ever pay tuition to listen to me lecture. And this morning, I'm considering jumping out the window here instead of going to class."

Professor Clark smiled. His cohorts raised their eyebrows. Perhaps I wasn't the first neophyte to have this reaction on the second day of school. I hoped he would offer some sage advice. Something profound. Something learned. Something—well—professorial. Something I could learn from and use to be a better professor of law. Instead, all he said was, "The dean's office here is on the first floor, y'know. If you jumped, you'd accomplish nothing."

It was now 7:50 a.m. and time for him to leave for his classroom and for me to do the same. He nodded, satisfied that he had handled the issue succinctly, and left for his classroom. His cohorts left, leaving me alone at the urn. I lingered. I resigned myself to the fact that I might just have to jettison the whole jumping notion. I would just have to tough it out, work harder at teaching, and get better.

❧

Just before finals time, the law students anonymously filled out a form and rated the class. Sixty-four potential critics whose reviews went to the dean for analysis and a determination of whether the adjunct professor—me—should stay on.

Sixty-three of them filled out the form and were kind, even encouraging. One review, written by student number sixty-four, however, stuck with me for all fourteen years of my teaching career. That one budding attorney wrote, "Someone should teach this guy how to teach."

Thankfully, she or he was in the distinct minority, but it hit too close to home for a rookie adjunct professor. I didn't have the confidence (yet) to brush off such a comment and go with the favorable reviews from the other sixty-three students. The hovering me didn't reappear, but the review was a gut punch in the fifteenth round of a boxing match.

Eight words. Short. Precise. Straight to the point. Pull no punches. Cut like a knife. Get in and get out delivery.

In retrospect, if I graded the review, I would have had to give this student an A for writing ability. I'm not sure what grade I would have given for developing a legal strategy that called out a professor, even an adjunct, to his face, even if the review was anonymous. Then again, it's a free country. She or he should be free to speak their truth.

But I remember accepting that "this person will make a brilliant attorney someday. Maybe a trial attorney?" I wonder if she or he did.

Wrapping It Up

58
Tying It All Together

Just this chapter and the next and you're done. You've made it this far. Thank you. I've made it this far in the book and in life. Thanks to my family, friends, and acquaintances for hanging in there with me in both endeavors. I've managed to get on with it in my life and you've managed to get on with it as well if you've made it to this chapter.

But now it's time to wrap it up. All things (good and bad) must end.

Before we get to the last chapter, maybe you're wondering, how is all this randomness connected?

Simply put, the stories are a microcosm of my life. They mirror it. They ramble around from event to event, story to story, idea to idea. All random. All unpredictable. All unplanned. All without a reliable roadmap. Because my life has been everything unplanned that happened after I planned everything out so carefully. My stories are my day-to-day existence. They're my relationship with life. They're inside my head, and now, outside it as well.

Now you've gotten a glimpse. The inside and the outside. The good and the bad.

Now you know what my head thinks and how it sorts things out—when it can. When it wants to.

I hope it wasn't too shocking or jarring. I hope it was funny, sad, and provocative. Thanks for the therapy sessions. Send me a bill.

If you decide to review the book, thank you very much. Also, please remember the difference between a critical review and mean-spirited criticism.

But most importantly, enjoy the next chapter—my last essay for now. To me, it's the most significant one in this book and certainly the most important one for me. As you read it, remember that through it all, I count myself lucky. Maybe the luckiest. As Bill Russell said, "To love someone is nothing, to be loved by someone is something, to love someone who loves you is everything." I've got that in spades. I try to remember it every day.

59

Ralph Waldo Got It Right (Be Yourself)

"To be yourself in a world that is constantly trying to make you something else is the greatest accomplishment."

– Ralph Waldo Emerson.

I DON'T KNOW if my dad ever read Emerson. I did in college. I was an American Studies major, and Emerson was required reading. We had talked before. Or, more accurately, he had tried to talk, and I wasn't ready. Now it was time. By the time my dad convened this important meeting with me, I was a senior. 1976.

We sat on the front porch of his small split-level house as the sun dipped below the horizon. He slowly inhaled his unfiltered Pall Mall, held the smoke in his lungs, and then purposefully exhaled. Like a smoke-filled sigh. He shook his head and pondered the smoldering cigarette between his tobacco-stained pointer and middle fingers. He would stop on Monday, he vowed to himself for the millionth time.

He came right to the point. "What's your thinking about the rest of your life? You have a plan?" he asked.

To have a plan, I needed *to* plan. Not my strong suit back then. *Rest of my life?* I sweated. *Seriously?* It was a heavy question to ask a twenty-year-old. I was just a kid.

But he asked, and he was my dad; he deserved an answer. At that point, I didn't feel my dad was trying to make me into "something else." He was trying to help me sort through this life decision. Or so I assumed. We agreed to reschedule the meeting to give me time to organize my ideas.

I came up with a Plan A and a Plan B to present to him in a few days. In "A," I'd be a professional photographer and take pictures for a living. Sports. I'd follow the New York Mets around the country for the *New York Times* or the *New York Daily News*.

In "B," I'd take a couple of years off after college and write. You know. The not-so-great American novel.

Maybe I'd do both "A" and "B." I was excited. I had plans.

I practiced my presentation and then we reconvened. I delivered Plans A and B. He sat quietly, arms folded, and listened. When I finished talking, he didn't need time to consider his response. Neither plan survived his scrutiny. He rejected both. "Pipe dreams," he said as he shook his head and sent me back to ponder some more.

I guess he wondered how he could've sent me to this fancy liberal arts college only to come up with Plans A and B.

I worried he had concluded my college years had been a waste of time. By then, I had changed my mind. He wasn't trying to guide me. He was on a path to make me into "something else."

I tried to come up with other plans and failed. After due consideration, I had no other ideas. So, I deferred my response, much to his chagrin, graduated from college, and drove a forklift for a while. Trouble was—as I've reported to you—I wasn't good at it.

Finally, I decided on law school. My dad was ecstatic. An attorney in the family.

But I assumed I wasn't going to law school to be an attorney, as

What Makes Me . . . Me

I've written before. The truth was, I went because it gave me three more years in the safe haven of law school to figure it all out. This part of the plan I didn't share with my dad. I spared my dad the truth because he couldn't handle that truth.

After law school, I clerked for a bankruptcy judge and then spent four decades in the business bankruptcy trenches practicing my trade. The years flew by until one day, I awoke and decided that writing was still very important. I still had it in me to write the not-so-great American novel. Or, as it turns out, four of them (so far), one memoir, and now this book of essays.

These days, I reflect on my path from time to time.

For years and years, I took his "pipe dream" comment as the first in a long line of events that seemed like attempts, some successful, by my dad and others to make me "something else." Maybe the world was well-meaning, but there are consequences when you try to make someone "something else."

The subject of your efforts may lose accountability. I did. If something went wrong, all I had to do was blame the world for steering me down the wrong path. And I blamed the world.

Damn world.

The years have now made me wiser, and once again, I don't imagine my dad was trying to make me "something else" way back in 1976. All he was doing was looking out for me, protecting his investment, guiding a youngster, advising an offspring, and providing free mentoring services. And trying to head off what he must've feared was going to be a colossal mistake. "*Writing?*" he probably worried. "What an insane idea."

In my wise older age, I realize he was correct if one is trying to be practical. But being practical is unnecessary for a not quite twenty-one-year-old. It's a time for some measure of exploration. Dreaming. And career elimination.

During my law career, I always had two lives: the life of what I wanted to do, which I pursued when I could and certainly not full-time, and the life of what the rest of the world had me do—try cases in bankruptcy court, which I mostly did full-time.

But now, I've achieved most of Emerson's wise observation, and I'm mostly myself. It is, as Emerson noted, in the category of "greatest accomplishment" for me, and it has the added benefit of putting a smile on my face daily.

I don't follow the Mets around the country with my cameras in hand, to be sure. But I shoot lots of sports (with a smile) and I write a good number of books (with a smile). I recognize none of them are the great American novel, but that's also okay.

Not everyone can be great. But, everyone should have the chance to pull off a great accomplishment or two. Thank you, Ralph Waldo.

Acknowledgments

Thanks and gratitude to:

Everyone who has has come and gone in my life for whatever reasons. If you've found this book on the shelves, reach out to me. Let's go back from "gone from my life" to "present and accounted for."

Debbie Burke for all her editing assistance, and Damon Freemon and the entire *Damonza* crew for their usual wonderful cover, formatting, and now proofreading, all helping to bring IW3M to life.

Veronica Yager of *Journey Bound Publishing* for all her indie author help and advice.

Patrick Hughes for learning what makes me . . . me and helping me be . . . me over the years.

Mark Foster for seeing me over the years and tolerating me.

The Shaikens for loving me over the years.

Jason DeWitt Photography for the great back cover portrait that captured part of me.

Emily and Loren for letting me run out of the room whenever and wherever to write and edit and who knows what else.

Henry Cox and Dallas Jones, my writing buddies, counselors, therapists, and friends. Always remember the difference between a writer and a pizza.

Dr. Ryan Caufield for giving me a partial new knee while I wrote IW3M. Ice on the knee. Fingers on the keyboard. Pu Erh nearby. Some Advil. Perfect.

And to you, for reading my book(s).

About the Author

Mark Shaiken lives with his wife, Loren, and their dog, Emily, in Denver, Colorado. He schooled at Haverford College and Washburn University and practiced commercial bankruptcy law for decades before moving on in 2019 to write, volunteer, travel, and play music.

In addition to his award-winning memoir (of a not-famous lawyer), *And . . . Just Like That: Essays on a Life Before, During, and After the Law*, he is the author of four books in his award-winning 3J legal thriller series: *Fresh Start, Automatic Stay, Unfair Discrimination,* and *Cram Down*. He will shortly begin work on the fifth in the series, *For Cause*.

Connect with Mark at *http://markshaikenauthor.com*.

Review Request

You would make an author happy if you would please leave a short review of *It's What Makes Me . . . Me* on Amazon, Goodreads, or wherever else you fill your reading pleasure.

In the My Library

It's What Makes Me . . . Me
Cram Down, https://tinyurl.com/3svm9f3x
Unfair Discrimination, https://tinyurl.com/5n8c4jtn
Automatic Stay, https://tinyurl.com/4pmvt44y
Fresh Start, https://tinyurl.com/49dkfs7w
And . . . Just Like That: Essays on a Life Before, During and After the Law, https://tinyurl.com/mr3tbka2
Automatic Stay Litigation in Bankruptcy (coauthored with Cindi Woolery), *https://tinyurl.com/9hh9bdz3*
Mark Shaiken Amazon Author Page, *https://tinyurl.com/3jb4xetn*
Mark Shaiken : : Author Web Page, *https://markshaikenauthor.com*

Manufactured by Amazon.ca
Bolton, ON